ILLUSTRATED HISTORY OF
WORLD WAR II

IAN BECKETT

ILLUSTRATED HISTORY OF
WORLD
WAR II

Portland House
A Division of Crown Publishers, Inc.

A Bison Book

This 1988 edition published by Portland House, distributed by Crown Publishers, Inc.
225 Park Avenue South
New York, NY 10003

Produced by
Bison Books Corp.
15 Sherwood Place
Greenwich, CT 06830
USA

Printed in Italy

Library of Congress Cataloging-in-Publication Data
Beckett, I. F. W. (Ian Frederick William)
Illustrated History of World War II/by Ian Beckett.
p.   cm.
ISBN 0-517-65842-9
1. World War, 1939-1945   I. Title
D743.B384 1988
940.53— dc19   87-34788
       CIP

ISBN 0-517-65842-9
h g f e d c b a

Printed in Italy

PAGE 1: The youthful face of Hitler's new order in Germany – a girl belonging to the Nazi Party's youth league and a stern-faced soldier.

PAGES 2-3: US jeeps are loaded onto landing craft as part of the preparations for the invasion of Normandy, June 1944.

PAGES 4-5: Two Hawker Hurricanes from the RAF's No 501 (City of Gloucester) Squadron take off to intercept a formation of German aircraft during the height of the Battle of Britain.

Contents

The first of the twentieth century's two global wars – that between 1914 and 1918 – was a catastrophic experience for Europe. It has been estimated that World War I resulted in some two million deaths with a further 20 million maimed or wounded, five million women were left widows, nine million children were left orphans and ten million left homeless refugees. In Britain, nine percent of all males under the age of 45 were killed, while in France something like ten percent of the total population died. Moreover, there were an estimated 27 million deaths worldwide from the Spanish influenza pandemic of 1918-19, the highest mortality rates being recorded in countries far from the main theaters of the war – such as the United States and India. Historians differ on the precise demographic impact of the conflict but it is undeniable that war losses could be perceived as casting long shadows in political terms. In France, for example, draconian laws were introduced against birth control and abortion, while the psychological impact of the losses sustained in World War I undoubtedly played a part in France's complete military collapse in the summer of 1940. Similarly, the fervent desire that there should be 'no more Sommes' colored British foreign policy in the 1930s.

The war had destroyed four empires – those of Imperial Germany, Austria-Hungary, Czarist Russia and Ottoman Turkey. In sweeping away so much of the old European order the war had also released political, social and economic tensions that were to have the profoundest consequences for the future. In political terms, the war marked the triumph of the nation-state. Under the influence of the American President, Woodrow Wilson, national self-determination was a guiding principle for the peace settlements but, in creating a host of new states, the treaties were to leave a disastrous legacy of frustrated national minorities and artificial unions that were collections of weaknesses rather than concentrations of strength. Whatever Wilson thought to the contrary, the other victorious Allied powers rejected any thought that self-determination applied outside Europe, but the aspirations of subject peoples could not be confined.

The British, whose empire reached its greatest extent in 1919 with the acquisition of former German colonies and the custody of new Middle Eastern states, encountered nationalist agitation in such areas as Ireland, India and Palestine. The Dominions, too, had confirmed their own national identities during the war to the extent that they secured separate representation from Britain at both Versailles and at the Washington Naval Conference in 1921. Britain could no longer be absolutely sure that Canada, Australia or South Africa would automatically follow London's lead and British foreign policy was conducted with at least half an eye on likely Dominion reaction to political events.

Beyond Europe, of course, the war had transformed the United States into a global power even if it chose to retreat

BELOW: A Nazi rally in Dresden, 1932. The large and enthusiastic crowd shows the growing popularity of the National Socialist movement.

BOTTOM: Hitler and other leading Nazis, including Goebbels (right), attend a Nazi rally.

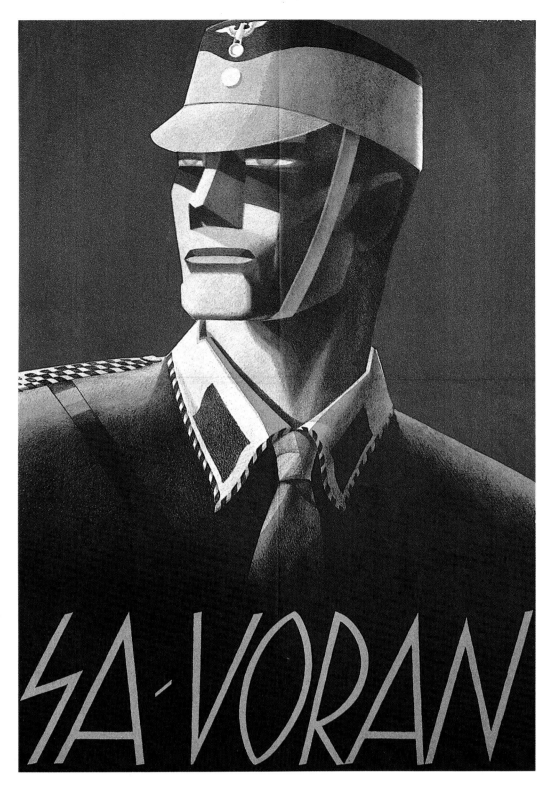

ABOVE: A Nazi propaganda poster of the SA, Hitler's personal security force.

FAR RIGHT: Joseph Stalin pictured at a meeting to commemorate the completion of the Moscow underground.

of the Red Army in Poland during 1920 barred communism's way to the West. Nevertheless, it was fear of Soviet communism that in part blinded Britain and France to the more immediate dangers posed by the re-emergence of Germany and the spread of Fascism throughout Europe, the latter emerging in the wake of frustrated nationalism, and the impact of defeat and a general disillusionment with democracy. Europe became a battlefield between the extremes of right and left, each sharing a loathing for existing democratic institutions which proved incapable of dealing with either the economic disasters of the interwar period or the threat these extremists posed to the *status quo*.

Economic problems were themselves a legacy of the war. There was a global depreciation in the value of currencies, which had the effect of destabilizing economies, and also a decentralization of the international economy. Europe's share of world production and trade fell through the development of non-European competition. The United States thus moved from being an international debtor before 1914 to an international creditor on a large scale. The war accelerated the economic challenge to Europe's primacy and the resulting economic depression only added to the appeal of political extremism. In short, Europe in the interwar years was in crisis and drifted, perhaps almost inevitably, into a second war which would become global like the first but one with even more far-reaching repercussions.

into international political isolation for another 20 years. It had also created at least an outward form of a new internationalism and world order in the shape of the League of Nations which was supposedly established to repudiate the 'secret diplomacy' of the old alliance systems of the past with 'open covenants of peace, openly arrived at.' Ironically, the war had also shattered the sense of international solidarity striven for by prewar socialists, the existing social democratic parties mostly succumbing to patriotism in 1914. Subsequently, the war brought 'respectability' to patriotic social democrats but divided them from those socialists who were dazzled by the prospects opened up by the one successful socialist revolution brought about by war. Lenin's successful *coup d'etat* in November 1917 polarized the Labor Movement and, thereafter, the proselytizing aspect of Russia's communism through its deliberate appeal to 'workers' over the heads of the 'ruling classes' was as much a danger to democratic socialists as to capitalist governments.

Fear of communism resulted in the creation of a *'cordon sanitaire'* of small states in eastern Europe. Events were to show that the fear of communism's contagion was exaggerated but it was still real and communist insurgencies had to be faced in Germany and Hungary before the defeat

CHAPTER ONE

HITLER'S RISE TO POWER

An alleged attack by Polish soldiers on a German frontier post took place on the evening of 31 August 1939. In reality, the incident was staged by the German *Schütz-staffel* (SS) and at 0430 on 1 September the German Luftwaffe struck at Polish airfields while five German armies plunged across the frontiers. General von Kluge's Fourth Army and General von Küchler's Third Army – both in General von Bock's Army Group North – advanced on Graudenz and Warsaw respectively. The Eighth (General Blaskowitz), Tenth (General von Reichenau) and Fourteenth Armies (General List) of General von Rundstedt's Army Group South aimed at Lodz, Warsaw and Kracow. There had been no declaration of war.

Caught by surprise despite the long period of tension that had preceded the attack, the Poles were confronted with the first demonstration of modern Blitzkrieg, combining devastating close air support from dive bombers with the mobility of the panzer divisions concentrated in the Fourth and Tenth Armies. While the campaign did not go entirely to plan and revealed both disparities between the mobility of the panzers and the rest of the army, and also many logistic failings, the Poles were unable to repel the onslaught. Kluge's and Küchler's forces linked to cut the Polish Corridor separating East Prussia from the remainder of Germany on 3 September, despite gallant resistance which had included pitting Polish horsed cavalry against German tanks. Six days later, the German XVI Panzer Corps was in the suburbs of Warsaw although that city was not to capitulate until 27 September. Elsewhere, 52,000 Polish troops were trapped around Kutno. On 17 September Russian troops poured into eastern Poland to seal the country's fate, and the foreign ministers of the Soviet Union and Germany met in Moscow on the 28th to divide the country between them. At the cost of nearly 46,000 casualties, the Germans had swept aside an army with a theoretical fully mobilized strength of 1.7 million in less than four weeks. But in the process Germany had initiated a world war, for on 3 September Britain and France had declared war.

In a very real sense, the seeds had been sown 20 years earlier in Germany's defeat at the end of World War I. The Treaty of Versailles signed on 28 June 1919 sought to prevent future conflicts on the same scale by banning secret treaties, expressing the hope that there would be global

PREVIOUS PAGES: Hitler salutes a march of supporters during an early Nazi rally at Nuremburg in August 1927. Rudolf Hess, his deputy, stands to Hitler's right in the car.

ABOVE: Members of the SA, armed with World War I weapons, in Neustadt during the abortive Nazi putsch of 1923.

LEFT: Members of the Freikorps patrol the streets of Berlin in an armored car during the political unrest of January 1919.

RIGHT: Nazi supporters litter the streets near Berlin's Brandenburg Gate with propaganda leaflets in March 1924.

ABOVE RIGHT: Communists are rounded up by the SA in Berlin following the Nazi-sponsored Reichstag fire of March 1933.

reduction in armaments, and in creating the League of Nations to defuse crises through discussion or collective action by its members against aggressors. But at the same time, Versailles and the linked treaties of St Germain (which dealt with Austria), Neuilly (which dealt with Bulgaria) and Trianon (which dealt with Hungary) imposed a new structure of states in central and eastern Europe. The Austro-Hungarian Empire was dismembered and two entirely new states were created – Yugoslavia and Czechoslovakia. Germany lost territory to both Czechoslovakia and a reborn Polish state to which Poznan, Upper Silesia and West Prussia were transferred together with the port of Danzig in order to give the Poles access to the sea. Alsace-Lorraine, which Germany had seized from France in 1871, was returned to France and the French were also permitted to enjoy the industrial production of the Saar, now to be administered by an International Commission for 15 years. Germany also lost her overseas colonies in Africa and the Pacific and smaller areas to Belgium and Denmark. Her armed forces were restricted to a strength of 100,000 men with weapons such as tanks, submarines and aircraft prohibited. Germany was also faced with economic reparations of 132 billion gold marks and branded as responsible for the war in the so-called War Guilt Clause.

In redrawing the map of Europe and in visiting retribution on the defeated, Versailles had created more problems than it had solved. Europe now had a series of states

containing substantial alien minorities, both Czechoslovakia and Yugoslavia in particular faced difficult problems of reconciling one nationality with another. Other states which had lost heavily such as Hungary, Bulgaria, and Germany had a vested interest in the future dismantling of the treaty provisions. Germany in particular had reason to resent the humiliation of Versailles. The German state – now the Weimar Republic – was hardly viable and could barely meet the massive reparations. The French reacted to Germany's failure to meet its outstanding debts by occupying the Ruhr in January 1923. Subsequently, a revised payment scheme – the Dawes Plan – was introduced by the Allies in September 1924 and was sufficiently agreeable for the French to leave the Ruhr in August 1925.

The resentments created by the treaties were to be exploited by political extremists. In Hungary, Admiral Miklos Horthy seized power in March 1920 and established a right-wing dictatorship. Similarly, anticommunist groups emerged in Italy whose territorial aspirations had not been met despite being one of the Allied powers during the war. A former journalist, Benito Mussolini, who had formed the *Fasci di Combattimento* in 1919, enjoyed increasing popular support. In October 1922 he led 25,000 of his supporters in a march to Rome and secured King Victor Emmanuel III's agreement to allow him to form a government and had soon assumed dictatorial powers. In Germany, one of the most active of the extremist groups was the National Socialist Party or Nazis, led from 1921 onward by an Austrian-born former wartime corporal in the German Army, Adolf Hitler. Hitler attempted a coup against the Bavarian state government in November 1923 proclaiming his Nazi revolution in a Munich beer hall. However, the affair was a fiasco and Hitler spent nine months in prison, setting down his political philosophy in a tract called *Mein Kampf* ('My Struggle').

Much of Hitler's ideology reflected traditional Germanic concerns, notably the desire to expand eastward to find *lebensraum* ('living space'), the active pursuit of which had been clearly demonstrated in the terms Germany had imposed on Russia and Rumania in the treaties of Brest-Litovsk and Bucharest in March 1918. At the time the war ended in November of that year, German troops were still pushing eastward in the hopes of carving out a German puppet state in the Ukraine and Crimea. Hitler's crude racialism also had its roots in traditional German and Austrian attitudes, while many shared his anticommunism. In January 1919 a communist rising in Berlin had been put down by right-wing paramilitaries known as Freikorps, who had also helped to defend the eastern frontier of the infant Weimar Republic against Poles, Balts, and Yugoslavs. The Republic's Army – the Reichswehr – had begun to rebuild for the future long before Hitler became of political account. Its Chief of Staff Hans von Seeckt designed the army in such a way that it could be rapidly expanded when opportunity offered – there were only 20,000 private soldiers but over 75,000 non-commissioned officers. The old German General Staff, abolished by the Allies, was carefully hidden among government civil offices. The Treaty of Rapallo signed with the Russians in 1922 also enabled the Reichswehr to undertake training with aircraft and tanks on Russian soil and out of sight of the Allied Control Commission, an arrangement which continued until 1935. Similarly, the German Navy kept abreast of submarine developments through a phony commercial company in the Netherlands.

Thus, the Nazis were able to strike certain chords in the popular imagination, and Hitler's charisma and pledges of future national recovery won increasing support. However, the catalyst for his climb to power proved to be the economic crisis of 1929 which reduced the other parties in the Weimar Republic's fragile democracy to impotence.

ABOVE: Germans, mainly women and children, search for scraps of food during the depression of 1923. Economic collapse, including rampant inflation, in the inter-war years drew many people to the Nazis.

The Social Democrats, who were the largest party in the Reichstag, left the coalition government in March 1930 rather than impose cuts in unemployment benefits. This instituted a crisis in which a minority government ruled only through presidential decree. In the September elections the Nazis made large gains, returning 107 representatives to the Reichstag on 18 percent of the popular vote. The size of the party's representation in the 608-seat assembly increased to 230 in the July 1932 election and ensured that no new government could be put together without the Nazis. However, the other parties resisted including Hitler in the government and another election had to be fought in January 1933. Nazi representation declined to 196 seats but President Hindenburg was persuaded to appoint Hitler as Chancellor because the army feared a communist uprising and civil war, and regarded having Hitler in government as a lesser evil. Hitler soon began consolidating his power, the communists being discredited by their supposed complicity in an arson attempt on the Reichstag in February 1933. This conve-

ABOVE: The beginning of the Nazi boycott of Jewish premises in Berlin on 1 April 1933. The posters order the public to avoid shopping in Jewish establishments.

ABOVE: *Hitler, accompanied by Himmler (left), the future leader of the SS, at the Nuremburg rally of 1934.*

ABOVE RIGHT: *The Italian dictator, Benito Mussolini. His dreams of an Italian empire included the conquest of Ethiopia.*

LEFT: *Shortly before his death, President Hindenburg attends a function in Berlin with Hitler, the German Chancellor, on 25 February 1934.*

RIGHT: *Italian troops enter the Ethiopian capital, Addis Ababa, on 5 May 1936. Despite their technological superiority, the Italians had great difficulty in subjugating the Ethiopians.*

niently allowed Hitler to get the two-thirds majority necessary for an Enabling Act to rule without parliament, and the Nazis secured 288 seats and 44 percent of the vote in the March elections. When Hindenburg died in August 1934 Hitler felt sufficiently strong enough to assume the presidency and proclaim himself *Führer*.

As the Nazi control of Germany increased so Hitler began to be more active in international affairs in an attempt to recover lost territories and to overturn Versailles. The announcement of German rearmament by Hitler in March 1935 blatantly transgressed the treaty. The League of Nations should have acted but it was a powerless organization. From the very beginning, the United States had declined to be a member and had withdrawn into international isolation in 1919. This left Britain and France as the only real guarantors of collective security since the League had no military forces and its success depended upon voluntary restraint. But both Britain and France faced their own domestic and imperial political and economic difficulties. Both were as suspicious of Soviet ambition in eastern Europe as of German ambition in central Europe and, in Britain at least, what became known as 'appeasement' reflected a certain feeling of guilt at Germany's poor treatment in 1919. Consequently, neither Britain nor France chose to give the League real teeth. In September 1931 the Japanese, with their own territorial ambitions in the Far East, invaded Manchuria, but the League responded with only ritual condemnation. Four years later an attempt to impose economic sanctions on Mussolini, who had revived Italy's interest in an East African empire by invading Ethiopia in October 1935, was equally ineffectual. Nor did the League try to intervene in the Spanish Civil War, which erupted in June 1936, despite the participation of Germans and Italians on the side of the Nationalists and of the Russians on the side of the Republicans. Republican defeat in April 1939 added another quasi-fascist state to the rapidly changing European political inventory.

Hitler and his Generals

Hitler could not have come to power without the acquiescence of the Reichswehr and the army was by no means as hostile to the Nazis as to the communists. Hitler's own war record was exemplary, he had the unique distinction of having won the Iron Cross First Class as an NCO. The Nazis had been careful to express due regard for the military and promised the expansion for which the army had long planned, consequently, early relations were cordial. This was due in no small way to the appointment of General Wernher von Blomberg as Reichswehr Minister on the day before Hitler became Chancellor. Known as *Gumme Löwe* ('Rubber Lion'), von Blomberg would certainly have been Hitler's choice for the position since he was so easily dominated. But his ability to keep on good terms with Hitler helped the army fend off challenges to its position from more unsavory elements in the Nazi Party including the SA, or Brownshirts. The army expressed little disquiet when Hitler eliminated the SA in the 'Night of the Long Knives' in June 1934 since it enabled it to expand unfettered.

Expansion was always the strongest link between party and army but it had the effect of undermining the officer corps; the 25,000 new officers commissioned between 1933 and 1939 were not drawn from traditional elites and did not share traditional values. It also awoke the uglier passions of ambition and opportunism among officers eager for promotion, and for this reason they were all the more willing to turn a blind eye to what was happening elsewhere in Germany. The man who became Army Commander in Chief in February 1934, General Freiherr Wernher von Fritsch, was alarmed at the pace of expansion but, like von Blomberg, welcomed it nonetheless. However, political instruction was introduced into the army in April 1934 and the notorious personal oath to the Führer four months later. Increasingly, von Fritsch and von Blomberg were worried by developments and in particular opposed any changes in the structure of the High Command and the forced pace of Hitler's foreign policy gambles. As a result, both were removed in February 1938, von Fritsch being framed for alleged homosexuality and von Blomberg forced to resign through his wife's alleged immorality.

Hitler now created a new supreme command, *Oberkommando der Wehrmacht* (OKW), with authority over the army (OKH), navy (OKM) and Luftwaffe (OKL) high command staffs and himself as Reichswehr Minister. Another compliant general, Field Marshal Walther von Brauchitsch became Army Commander in Chief while Wilhelm Keitel became Chief of Staff to OKW and Alfred Jodl his deputy. Another leading opponent of foreign policy objectives, the Army Chief of Staff General Ludwig Beck, resigned in August 1938 when he could not persuade his colleagues to take a collective stand against plans for Czechoslovakia. He was replaced by General Franz Halder. While Beck indulged in plotting – a projected coup failed to materialize in November 1939 through von Brauchitsch's indecisiveness – Halder engaged in procrastination. Thereafter, the army submitted to Hitler's whims despite the large number of generals sacked and the insults continually heaped upon it such as the introduction of the Nazi salute in July 1944. Indeed, between 1939 and 1945 no less than 22 German generals were executed and 110 committed suicide while 963 others died or disappeared while on active service.

Thus, there was little to dissuade Hitler from pressing ahead with his territorial revisionism. Germany left the League in October 1934 and in March 1936 re-occupied the Rhineland, which had been demilitarized in 1919 to form a buffer zone between France and Germany. Pre-occupied with Italian aggression in Ethiopia, Britain and France did not react – Italy was in fact a guarantor with them of the zone's demilitarization, as confirmed by the Treaty of Locarno in 1925. On 1 November 1936 Germany and Italy joined forces in the 'Rome-Berlin Axis' and Japan signed an 'Anti-Comintern Pact' with Germany on 25 November (the Comintern or Communist International being the agency through which the Soviets sought to export their brand of revolution). Hitler's next target was *Anschluss* – the union of Germany with Austria – which was again specifically prohibited by Versailles. On 12 March 1938 German troops marched into Austria before the Austrian government could carry out a planned ple-biscite on unification. Having removed opponents within the army – the Wehrmacht as it was now known – Hitler was free to move for the annexation of the Sudetenland, that part of Czechoslovakia lost at Versailles.

The Czechs were in no mood to accept humiliation and in April 1938 they mobilized when Germany moved troops up to the frontier in support of demands being made by Nazi sympathizers in the Sudetenland. Britain and France now appeared to be ready to support the Czechs, but in reality neither was in a position to fight a war for a distant country. The British Prime Minister Neville Chamberlain met Hitler twice in September 1938 seeking a solution, but Hitler would not be satisfied with only half the Sudeten-land, and at Munich on 29 September, Chamberlain and the French agreed to his demands. The Czechs had not been consulted but were compelled to comply as German forces entered the Sudetenland on 1 October. Other countries also seized their chance. The Poles took Teschen in October and the Hungarians claimed territory along their frontier with Czechoslovakia in November. As the Czech state disintegrated, the Ruthenes and Slovaks declared their independence in early 1939 and on 15 March Germany occupied what was left and the Hungarians occupied Ruthenia.

RIGHT: Neville Chamberlain returns to Hendon airfield to proclaim 'Peace in our Time' in September 1938, after a meeting with Hitler.

LEFT: Germany's Condor Legion parades before Hitler at the conclusion of the Spanish Civil War. German forces gained valuable combat experience in the conflict.

BELOW LEFT: A Bf-109, one of the Luftwaffe's best early-war fighters, of the Condor Legion in Spain.

BOTTOM, FAR LEFT: German troops enter the Rhineland to an enthusiastic welcome in 1936, regaining territory lost at the Versailles treaty.

BOTTOM LEFT: German mounted troops march into the former demilitarized zone of the Rhineland, a move which heightened international tension.

BELOW: Mussolini, Hitler, Dr Schmidt and Chamberlain discuss European affairs at Munich in September 1938.

Having shared in the spoils, the Poles realized that they would be the next target. But opinion had now shifted decisively against Hitler in Britain and France. Consequently, Chamberlain not only issued a guarantee to the Poles that they would be supported but, in April 1939, also reintroduced conscription in Britain. Hitler's own position had been strengthened immeasurably by the relatively bloodless foreign policy successes which had undermined those in the German armed forces alarmed at risking a war before Germany was ready. As early as October 1938 Hitler had begun to make demands on the Poles to return the Polish Corridor. He did get Lithuania to return Memel in March 1939 and extracted Rumanian agreement to supply Germany's oil needs. Nevertheless, the next act in the drama did not concern Germany but Italy, when Mussolini invaded Albania on 7 April 1939 in search of a Balkan empire. On 22 May Hitler and Mussolini signed a 'Pact of Steel' and on 23 August Hitler secured Soviet agreement to neutrality in a Non-Aggression Pact. It was also agreed by Hitler and the Soviet dictator Stalin to partition Poland when Hitler's attack began. It is possible that to the very last Hitler did not believe that Britain and France would fight for the Poles. However, it had always been his intention to neutralize the French at least before turning to the ultimate and decisive campaign against the Soviet Union.

Stalin had offered to help the western Allies at the time of Munich but his assistance had been discounted on both military and political grounds. Therefore, he had sought to guarantee Russian security by entering the Non-Aggression Pact with Hitler. At the same time, the Soviets' other flank was also secured by forcing the Japanese, whose forces were worsted by the Soviets in Mongolia, to leave the Anti-Comintern Pact. But Stalin also had other aims. Hitler had been prepared to concede a Soviet sphere of influence in the Baltic and in October 1939 the Soviets forced the tiny Baltic states of Latvia, Lithuania and Estonia to accept the entry of Russian troops. Then Finland, which like the others had wrested its independence from Russia during the Russian Civil War, was confronted by demands for a new frontier in Karelia and other areas. The Finns rejected the Soviet demands on 26 November 1939 and Soviet troops invaded four days later. Despite the tremendous disparity in numbers between their forces and

TOP LEFT: German Pzkpfw Mark II tanks push through a Polish forest.

ABOVE LEFT: German troops advance into a Polish town behind the cover of an armored car, September 1939.

LEFT: One of the feared Ju 87B Stukas over Poland. Air superiority allowed the Wehrmacht to move and attack at will in the short campaign.

ABOVE RIGHT: The taste of victory in the fallen city of Warsaw.

RIGHT: After the brief campaign Poland was partitioned between the forces of Nazi Germany and Soviet Russia. Here, nervous border guards pose for the camera.

ABOVE: *Finnish troops move through a town in eastern Karelia devastated by Soviet artillery fire, February 1940. Although outnumbered, the Finns inflicted heavy losses on the Soviet forces.*

RIGHT: *An armored car abandoned by the Red Army's 44th Division near Suomussalmi, Finland.*

ABOVE LEFT: *Russian troops dismantle Finnish anti-tank defenses near Teriiolii in Karelia during December 1939. The obstacles were part of the Mannerheim Line which, although incomplete, held the Red Army's early attacks.*

LEFT: *Finnish soldiers make use of a barricade of splintered timber during the Winter War.*

those of the Soviets, the Finns resisted throughout the winter months as the Soviets threw themselves vainly on the Mannerheim Line – named after the Finnish Commander in Chief. It was not until February 1940 that a new Soviet offensive broke through the Finnish defenses and on 12 March 1940 the Finns surrendered about 16,000 square miles of their territory in the Treaty of Moscow. But it had cost the Soviets an estimated 200,000 dead, and their abysmal showing persuaded the Germans that the Red Army was not a threat. The western Allies had been able to do little to help the Finns in the 'Winter War,' the League of Nations only stirring itself to expel the Soviet Union in December 1939 in one last meaningless gesture.

The Winter War was another demonstration of the inability of the Allies to intervene in a distant campaign and it was only perhaps at sea that the British and French could do much damage to Germany. But here, too, early successes were those of the Germans until the scuttling of the *Admiral Graf Spee* off Montevideo on 18 December 1939. But for the most part it was the 'Phony War' as the French sat solidly behind the Maginot Line facing the German Siegfried Line. However, Hitler feared that the Allies might seize the initiative and use the excuse of helping the Finns to occupy parts of Scandinavia. Norway was particularly important to Germany both as a possible naval base for operations in the Atlantic and also because vital Swedish iron ore was routed to Germany over Norwegian territory and down the Norwegian coast in the winter months when the Baltic was frozen. Hitler's fears were heightened by the Royal Navy's seizure of the German supply ship *Altmark* in Norwegian waters on 16

February 1940 and he decided to invade Norway, an operation soon expanded to include Denmark as well.

While Denmark could be seized by airborne and land assault, Norway had to be conquered from the sea. All ports were to be seized simultaneously by forces sailing in utmost secrecy. In fact, the German task force heading for

ABOVE: *The German pocket battleship* Graf Spee *in flames off Montevideo.*

LEFT: *Happier days for the* Graf Spee, *seen here on a prewar cruise.*

The Battle of the River Plate

Commanded by Captain Hans Langsdorf, the *Admiral Graf Spee* left Wilhelmshaven on 23 August 1939 for its wartime cruising station in the south Atlantic. Langsdorf received authorization to begin commerce raiding on 26 September and claimed his first victim – the British vessel *Clement* off Pernambuco in Brazil four days later. After destroying another eight merchantmen in a voyage that included a foray into the Indian Ocean, *Graf Spee* was moving westward toward the estuary of the River Plate when on 13 December she sighted what was assumed to be a convoy. The convoy turned out to be the British cruisers *Exeter*, *Ajax*, and *Achilles* comanded by Commodore H H Harwood. Langsdorf decided to attack and the action opened at 0617. *Exeter* closed on the German ship to draw her fire while *Ajax* and *Achilles* maneuvered to the

flanks. By 0740 when *Ajax* and *Achilles* broke off the battle, *Exeter* had been completely knocked out of action and *Ajax* was also badly damaged, but Langsdorf unexpectedly retired toward Montevideo in Uruguay. The *Graf Spee* had received 17 hits during the exchanges but none had caused serious damage and there were only 94 casualties in the crew of 1100. Possibly Langsdorf was unnerved by being knocked unconscious at one stage during the action for he appeared to believe that the superficial damage done made his ship unseaworthy. The British engaged in considerable bluff to keep *Graf Spee* in Montevideo until they could bring up naval reinforcements and on 17 December *Graf Spee* was scuttled by her crew when ordered out of Uruguayan waters. Langsdorf committed suicide three days later.

Narvik was discovered quite by chance on 8 April 1940 by Royal Navy vessels laying mines, but the Norwegians were slow to react and the Germans still achieved considerable surprise at Narvik, Oslo, Bergen, Kristiansand and Trondheim on the following day. German airborne troops also seized Sola and Stavangar. While Denmark fell in a single day, its king anxious to avoid useless bloodshed, the Norwegians fought back stubbornly. Coastal batteries at Oslo sank the German cruiser *Blücher* and damaged the pocket battleship *Lützow*. It became something of a race between German reinforcements and hastily organized Allied relief forces who landed at the minor ports of Namsos and Aandalsnes to try and recapture Trondheim. Unfortunately for the Allies, the Germans were able to use captured Danish and Norwegian airfields to achieve air superiority over Norway and the expeditionary force was forced out of Aandalsnes on 2 May and from Namsos on the following day. Allied efforts were more successful at Narvik which was taken by British, French, and Polish forces on 28 May 1940 but they were also forced to withdraw on 8 June by events in France and the Low Countries. The Norwegian Army finally capitulated to the Germans on 9 June.

The attempt to help the Norwegians had not been wholly disastrous for the Allies. Casualties had been light with some 4000 on the Allied side and 5000 on the German side, but at least some damage had been inflicted on the German Navy. It would also ultimately prove costly for Hitler in terms of the manpower he continued to retain in Norway throughout the war for fear of Allied counterinvasion. However, the effective loss of Norway by early May and the apparent bad management of the campaign provoked a governmental crisis in Britain and led to Chamberlain's resignation on 9 May. The man who had been brought back from the political wilderness as First Lord of the Admiralty in September 1939 was now invited by the king to form a new government. A long-standing prophet of the dangers posed by German rearmament, Winston Churchill took up the reins on the very day that the German Blitzkrieg opened in France and the Low Countries – 10 May 1940.

ABOVE: German infantry, led by a Panzer II, pause by a burning village in Norway before resuming their advance in March 1940.

ABOVE LEFT: Winston Churchill, the charismatic leader of Britain's wartime government, pictured in May 1940.

LEFT: German troops embark for the invasion of Norway. Despite British and French military support, the Norwegians surrendered to the invaders in June 1940.

RIGHT: Crippled shipping lies in the harbor of Narvik in Norway, April 1940.

CHAPTER TWO

BLITZKRIEG IN THE WEST

Hitler had ordered an offensive against the West to be planned on 9 October 1939 and within ten days the German High Command had presented the first version of its *Plan Gelb* (Plan Yellow). This was similar to the Schlieffen Plan of 1914 in envisaging a flanking move through neutral Belgium which would amount to little more than the occupation of the Low Countries. However, when a German plane carrying the plans crash landed at Mechelen in Belgium on 10 January 1940, it gave the opponents of the original plan the opportunity to press for significant changes. In particular, the Chief of Staff to Army Group A, General von Manstein, argued that it would be possible to stage a major armored breakthrough across the seemingly impenetrable Ardennes to the north of the Maginot Line and to drive to the Channel coast. With the backing of his army commander, General von Rundstedt, von Manstein was able to win agreement to the change of plan on 27 February. Thus, 44 German divisions of von Rundstedt's Army Group, including seven of the ten Panzer divisions, were concentrated opposite the Ardennes which were held by 12 second-rate divisions of elderly French Territorials. Von Bock's Army Group B in the north with 28 divisions would act, in the words of the British historian Basil Liddell Hart, as a 'matador's cloak' to draw off the Allied forces from the decisive point. The 17 divisions of von Leeb's Army Group C in the south would advance against the Maginot defenses.

The Allies assumed that the Germans would attempt to repeat the Schlieffen maneuver with the main weight of their offensive coming through Belgium. Consequently, the French High Command intended to advance to meet the Germans in Belgium and had envisaged doing so ever since 1920. The Belgians' understandable reluctance to see their country used as a French battlefield had been one factor in Belgium's declaration of neutrality in October 1936 which meant that there could be no official co-ordination of military plans prior to the German invasion. Of necessity, the British Expeditionary Force (BEF) was also committed to an advance into Belgium when talks began between the British and French staffs in March 1939 and Plan D or the Dyle Plan of October 1939 designated 35 Allied divisions for an advance to the line of the River Dyle with a further nine in reserve. A total of 43 French divisions were to hold the Maginot Line while the uncommitted elements of the French general reserve comprised just ten divisions for the whole front from Switzerland to the sea.

The Allies had superiority over the Germans in terms of the number of divisions (135 to 114) and in tanks. The French had 4688 tanks, of which 3254 were in the north or northeast, as opposed to a German total of 3862 tanks, of which only 2574 were in the same sector. French tanks were also more heavily armored and better gunned than German tanks. What mattered, however, was that whereas German armor was highly concentrated, French strategic thought interpreted the tank as a weapon for infantry support to be distributed in penny packets. There were only three armored divisions and three light mechanized divisions in the French order of battle, the former newly raised and all in reserve and the latter all earmarked for the Belgium option. The British Army had only 310 tanks in France in May 1940 in light-armored regiments and the 1st Army Tank Brigade, its 1st Armored Division being committed to the south only after the German offensive had begun. On 10 May, therefore, as the Germans swept into Holland and Belgium, the Allies conformed to the Dyle Plan with the French 1st Army Group under General Billotte advancing into Belgium. In theory, General Lord Gort's BEF was also under Billotte's command. In practice Gort received directions from the French Commander in Chief, General Gamelin, through the agency of the headquarters at La Ferté-sous-Jouarre of the Northeast Front commanded by General Georges. Matters were further complicated by the discretion allowed Gort by the British government to appeal direct to London against any of Georges' orders which appeared to 'imperil the British Field Force.' Gamelin, who was also French Army Chief of Staff, at Vincennes, was also forced to share a common staff with Georges: it was located approximately 20 miles from both of their headquarters, at Montry.

By the evening of 11 May the German 9th Panzer Division had linked up with paratroopers dropped at Moerdijk on the first day of the offensive. Deventer, Arnhem and Nijmegen had all fallen on that first day and Dutch resistance crumbled following the bombing of Rotterdam on 14 May. The Dutch surrendered at 1145 on the 15th and Giraud's French Seventh Army, which had moved to their assistance, was forced back into Belgium. Airborne attack had similarly paralyzed the Belgian defenses, the key and supposedly impregnable fort at Eben Emael on the Albert canal fell to glider-borne troops in barely an hour. Agreement was hastily reached between the French, British, and Belgians on 12 May to co-ordinate the Allied forces in Belgium under Billotte's direction, but there was little opportunity for him to do so and he was fatally injured in a car crash nine days later. By that time the failure of the

PREVIOUS PAGES: British Bren-gun carriers wait to advance, while French troops and civilians retreat, May 1940.

RIGHT: German infantry advance through the shell-blasted streets of a town in the Low Countries.

BELOW RIGHT: Dutch infantry put up a gallant but doomed resistance to the invader. Much of their equipment was outdated by German standards.

The Maginot Line

Following France's grievous losses of manpower in the Great War, both soldiers and politicians were agreed on the need to adopt a primarily defensive strategy in any future war by sheltering behind a 'continuous front' which would enable France to build up her strength for an eventual offensive. French strategic thought also embraced the value of 'couverture,' originally a thin screen of troops along a frontier able to give ample warning of the enemy's intentions but now extended to mean a sufficiently strong force to hold the frontier until reserves could be mobilized. In 1922 a special commission recommended a series of fortified zones, although they would have gaps for French offensives, and a further commission in 1926-7 recommended three such zones in Alsace, Lorraine, and around Belfort. However, the continuing manpower crisis resulted in the idea of using concrete as a substitute for troops and of closing any gaps in the fortified zones to produce a continuous front of fortifications. Named after the French minister of war, André Maginot, money for the frontier fortifications of the 'Maginot Line' was voted in January 1930. The drawback of the line was that it was not continuous but stopped 250 miles short of the coast; this was because the Ardennes were considered impenetrable, and much of the remainder too heavily populated and industrialized. Suggestions were made in 1933 to extend the fortifications farther north but these were rejected as the French increasingly envisaged launching an offensive through Belgium at the outbreak of any war.

Deserted bunkers of the 'impregnable' Maginot Line near Diedenhofner.

Eben Emael

At the northern extremity of Liége's modern defenses in Belgium, Eben-Emael commanded the bridges over the Albert Canal and thus the route to the west. Built between 1932 and 1935 the fortifications were masked by the canal cutting as well as by embankments, trenches and walls. Linked by a series of underground tunnels, the defenders manned a range of 7.5cm and 12cm cannon in cupolas. The German Sixth Army needed to take this apparently formidable obstacle in order to effect a breakthrough to the west. The only solution was to use glider-borne assault and a special Storm Detachment, commanded by Captain Koch, was assembled. Those tasked with the attack on Eben Emael were 85 men of the Sapper Detachment of the Parachute Infantry Battalion in 7th Airborne Division. The group under the command of First Lieutenant Rudolf Witzig trained for six months at Hildesheim and Köln, and on captured fortifications in the Sudentenland and Poland. Equipped with flamethrowers and special 50-kg cavity charges capable of penetrating up to 25cm of concrete, they were to land in four sections from 11 gliders at 0525 on 10 May 1940 – five minutes before the German Army crossed the Belgian frontier. Nine gliders landed on top of the fortifications but two, including that of Witzig, landed off course. The remaining teams blasted the cupolas and shafts and kept the 750 Belgian defenders underground until relieved by the 51st Sapper Battalion at 0700 on 11 May. The confused, shaken Belgians finally capitulated around noon that day, having lost 23 dead and 59 wounded. The German casualties were just six dead and 15 wounded.

LEFT: Hitler meeting the paratroopers who captured the Belgian frontier fortress of Eben Emael – Witzig (center) and Koch (right) – in May 1940.

RIGHT: Rommel's 7th Division sweeps across France, heading for the Channel.

BELOW RIGHT: German assault boats cross the River Meuse, the major barrier opposing the Wehrmacht's drive toward Sedan in the opening phase of the Blitzkrieg against France.

Dyle Plan had long been sealed by events farther south.

The leading elements of von Rundstedt's Army Group A had reached the Meuse at Sedan by 12 May, the Ardennes proving no obstacle to armor and the meager French defenses being pushed aside. With the support of a five-hour bombardment of French positions by Stuka dive bombers, troops of Guderian's XIX Panzer Corps crossed the Meuse in rubber boats in the early evening of 13 May to establish a bridgehead three miles wide and four to six miles deep. The nature of the French resistance in these crucial days is best represented by the example of the 55th Division at Sedan which had still lost only 40 dead by the end of May but had ceased to exist as a formation with its men having fled, gone missing, or been taken prisoner. Without sufficient air support, Reinhardt's XLI Panzer Corps was unable to force a crossing of the Meuse at Montherme for another three days, but Rommel's 7th Panzer Division in Hoth's XV Panzer Corps was able to force a crossing at Dinant. Allied aircraft failed to destroy the pontoons the Germans had flung across the river and a gap developed between the French Second and Ninth Armies which a hastily organized new Sixth Army could not plug. In the process, each of the three French armored divisions were fed into the battle piecemeal and all destroyed by the evening of 15 May. An *ad hoc* 4th Armored Division was put together under the command of Colonel Charles de Gaulle, who had long advocated the creation of armored formations in the French Army, but this too was swept aside on 17 May without noticeably slowing the impetus of the German advance.

In fact, the only real opposition to the exploitation of the breakthrough on the Meuse emanated from a German High Command increasingly nervous at the scale of the apparent success. General von Kleist, who had overall command of the panzers in Army Group A, had tried to halt Guderian on 15 May and again two days later, since it was feared that the belated appearance of the French armor heralded counterattacks on the exposed flanks of the advance. But French morale had all but collapsed; Prime Minister Reynaud telephoned Churchill on the morning of 16 May to announce that the battle had been

Blitzkrieg

The German concept of Blitzkrieg owed much to the assimilation of ideas from other countries. The Nazis studied the writings of pioneering armored warfare theorists such as J F C Fuller in Britain and Charles de Gaulle in France, and read the reports and manuals deriving from maneuvers with armored formations carried out in Britain in the 1920s. But at the same time, Blitzkrieg suited the desire for a new mobility harnessed to the traditional preference for the offensive, generated in the German Army in the 1920s, and it found a tireless advocate in the young Heinz Guderian. Appointed to the Inspectorate of Transport Troops in 1922, Guderian became convinced of the value of armor. In 1927 he was able to begin experimenting with mock tanks and was assisted both by the opening of a secret German tank school at Kazan in the Soviet Union that year and by the translation of a British manual in 1929. His own *Achtung Panzer* published in 1937 was an effective defense of armored warfare and, in the same year, a panzer army which did not yet exist was written into the German plans for action against Czechoslovakia. In November 1938 Guderian became Commander of Mobile Troops, Hitler's own interest having been aroused in the possibilities of a 'lightning war' which could secure foreign policy objectives at minimum cost and thus avoid undue strain on a weak economy.

Essentially, the tactics were similar to those outlined by Fuller in his 'Plan 1919' 20 years before. Characterized by its speed and psychological violence, the attack would rupture the enemy front at several points by using armor concentrated on a narrow frontage. Strongpoints would be by-passed in a 'mission of paralysis' to penetrate deeply into the enemy rear and dislocate the opposing command structure. The panzer divisions created to achieve this effect were all-arms formations with integral support for the tanks from motorized infantry and mechanized artillery. The importance of the Luftwaffe to Blitzkrieg should also be emphasized; experience gained during the Spanish Civil War showing the value of the Stuka dive bomber as flying artillery. Techniques had also been evolved in Spain for co-ordinating air and ground formations so that the Luftwaffe could provide tactical air support on the battlefield to maintain the attacking momentum. Blitzkrieg was not without its weaknesses, principally in placing too much emphasis on the initiative of individual commanders who almost engaged in competition with one another. In campaigns of longer duration than those of 1939 and 1940, the logistic shortcomings of the German Army would also become apparent. The Polish campaign showed the Mark II tank to be virtually useless for armored combat and the Mark III to be undergunned. The Mark IV was by far the best machine at the beginning of the war with a 7.5cm gun but German industry was not capable of meeting the demand, and it was only through pressing Czech chassis into service that losses were made good for the 1940 campaigns. Motorization had still not proceeded fast enough by the time the Germans invaded Russia in June 1941.

LEFT: *A captured French B2 tank. Although many of the French Army's tanks were superior, their deployment in penny packets led to heavy losses.*

RIGHT: *A British 2-pounder anti-tank gun crew defend a position amid the ruins of Louvain in Belgium, 14 May 1940.*

BELOW LEFT: *A German motorcycle reconnaissance unit from Rommel's 7th Division takes a break during the hectic pursuit of the retreating Allies.*

BELOW: *One of the most numerous tanks in the Wehrmacht's armored division of 1940 – the Pzkpfw Mark II. Although lightly protected and poorly armed, it had a high top speed.*

lost. The French government prepared to abandon Paris for Tours and Gamelin resolved to order the withdrawal of the French forces from Belgium. Subsequently, on the morning of 19 May he at last recognized the opportunity to attack the German flanks with the forces withdrawn from Belgium in the north and the remains of Second and Sixth Armies from the south. But it was now too late and Weygand, who had been ordered home from the Levant where he had been Commander in Chief since August 1939, replaced Gamelin that evening. Weygand, who had never commanded any formation above a brigade in battle, canceled Gamelin's orders. Meanwhile, the panzers had regrouped on 19 May and at 1900 on the 20th Guderian's 2nd Panzer Division swept into Abbeville.

The Allied situation was now critical, especially for Gort who had to decide whether to retire to the Channel ports or attempt to fight it out to the southwest. The BEF and the Belgians had not immediately been notified of Billotte's decision to withdraw from the Dyle to the Schelde on 15 May, and both armies were able to execute the maneuver only through the caution of von Bock's Sixth Army by then deprived of the support of XVI Panzer Corps

The Arras Counterattack, 21 May 1940

Designed to ease the German pressure on Arras and to delay any encircling movement around the BEF, the British attack at Arras aimed to clear the ground between the town and the Cojeul river but it was regarded primarily as a 'mopping up' operation against light German forces. An *ad hoc* force was assembled under the command of Major General Martel consisting of two tank battalions (4th and 7th Royal Tank Regiments), two infantry battalions (6th and 8th Durham Light Infantry) and some artillery and anti-tank batteries. The units involved had not served together before, signal communications between them were limited and, in the event, the artillery and infantry could not keep up with the tanks. The tanks themselves were limited in armament, the 58 Mark Is having only machine guns, although the 16 Mark IIs had

mounted 2-pounder guns. Commanding from an open car, Martel was unable to keep control when his force unexpectedly ran into elements of the German 7th Panzer and SS Totenkopf Divisions. Nevertheless, the surprise achieved and the virtual immunity conferred by the British tanks' thick frontal armor against German 37-mm anti-tank guns sowed the seeds of panic all the way up the German chain of command. The Germans only restored the situation by the evening by forming gun lines including 88-mm anti-aircraft guns and launching counterattacks with tanks supported by Stukas. The Germans lost only 30 tanks — British losses are unknown — but the attack had a considerable measure of success in delaying the sweeping German advance on Arras and in alarming the German High Command.

TOP LEFT: Heinz Guderian, one of the leading exponents of Blitzkrieg, keeps track of his leading armored elements in the breakout from Sedan.

ABOVE, FAR LEFT: Infantry, supported by Pzkpfw Mark IVs and 35ts of Guderian's command, move through open country during the Battle of France.

ABOVE: A Pzkpfw Mark IV with a low-velocity gun.

ABOVE LEFT: A Panzer column on the move.

LEFT: A British light tank causes a stir in a Belgian town.

RIGHT: A 4.7cm pak gun mounted on a Pzkpfw Mark I chassis.

which had been ordered south. The British War Cabinet ordered Gort to move southwestward on 20 May and restore the front, but he decided that this was impracticable with seven of his nine divisions engaged with the Germans, and proposed only to use the 5th and 50th Divisions around Arras in support of an anticipated French attack from the south. In the event, the French counterattack upon which Weygand had now decided broke down even before it began because of Billotte's death, although the British attack, by the 1st Tank Brigade and elements of the 5th and 50th Divisions, which fell largely on Rommel's division, caused momentary shock waves in the Panzer Group and in the Fourth Army. It also played some part in von Rundstedt's order to halt the panzers on 24 May when they were just 16 miles from Dunkirk. More important was the fact that 50 percent of von Kleist's armor was now out of action through mechanical or other breakdown and that the armor would be needed to spearhead any advance to the south. It was also assumed that the BEF was trapped and consequently Hitler endorsed the order. It was not reversed until 26 May by which time the British had had the opportunity to reinforce both Boulogne and Calais.

Meanwhile, continuing pressure by von Bock's forces on the Belgian front now caused Gort to take the courageous decision on 25 May to pull back the 5th and 50th Divisions from Arras and to reinforce the left flank in the knowledge that it implied retirement on the Channel ports. The start of the evacuation of troops (Operation Dynamo) was signaled by the Admiralty at 1857 on 26 May. The Allied retirement toward Dunkirk was assisted by the gallant defense of both Boulogne and Calais, which fell on 25th and 26th respectively; by the efforts of the 2nd,

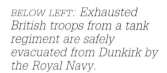

ABOVE: General Weygand, recalled to save France, was unable to stem the German tide.

RIGHT: German infantry shelter from French fire behind a wall before resuming their advance.

LEFT: As the Battle for France continues, German motorcycle troops advance through the Champagne country.

BELOW LEFT: Exhausted British troops from a tank regiment are safely evacuated from Dunkirk by the Royal Navy.

BELOW: German troops investigate an abandoned British Matilda infantry tank. Although lightly armed, its heavy armor was impervious to most anti-tank guns of the period.

5th, and 48th Divisions to keep open a corridor through which the rest of the BEF could retreat, and the French defense of Lille. The Belgians also attempted to win additional time but were finally forced to surrender at 2300 hours on the 28th.

By 29 May, however, much of the BEF and almost half of the French First Army had attained the relative security of the perimeter at Dunkirk from which large numbers of support troops had already been evacuated successfully. With the German High Command more concerned with continuing their offensive to the south, it was largely left to the Luftwaffe to finish off the BEF. The Royal Navy itself expected that only 45,000 men would escape. In fact, in an extraordinary epic of improvisation, over 850 vessels of all shapes and sizes evacuated 338,226 men from the beaches, of whom 139,067 were Belgian or French troops. The last ship left at 0340 on 4 June. The BEF had suffered 68,111 casualties and lost most of its equipment but had escaped to fight again.

But Dunkirk was not the end of the Battle for France. Weygand called for a last stand on the Somme on 26 May and created a new quadrillage or 'hedgehog' system of defense with infantry and artillery using natural obstacles as the basis for strongpoints and company-sized *Groupes Franc* utilizing remaining tanks to block main roads. The weakness was the lack of tactical aircraft and armor to effect adequate counterattacks around the strongpoints. The Germans reorganized, with von Rundstedt given 45 divisions (including four panzer divisons) to attack east of

BELOW: German troops experiment with an assault craft for Operation Sealion, the planned invasion of Britain.

LEFT: German troops, including machine-gunners, take shelter behind a wall in a French street and watch for snipers.

RIGHT: The Battle for France, showing the rapid advance of the Wehrmacht.

BELOW, FAR LEFT: A German 37mm anti-tank gun is used against a strongpoint during the Battle for France.

BELOW, FAR RIGHT: The crew of a German light mortar in action. One man prepares the bomb; the other lines up on a target.

GREAT BRITAIN

DOVER

BELGIUM

Army Group B

Pz Group Kleist

Army Group A

Hoth
XV Pz
Corps

XIV Pz
Corps

XVI Pz
Corps

Second and
Ninth Armies

GERMANY

ENGLISH CHANNEL

Somme

ABBEVILLE

CHERBOURG

ST VALÉRY
FÉCAMP

DIEPPE

AMIENS

PERONNE

Pz Group Guderian

SEDAN

LUX.

LE HAVRE

Fr Tenth Army

XXXIX Pz
Corps

XLI Pz
Corps

Army Group C

CAEN

ROUEN

Fr Seventh
Army

RETHEL

Fr
Second Army

Channel
Islands

Oise

Fr Sixth
Army

RHEIMS

VERDUN

METZ

Maginot Line

BREST
19 June

PARIS
14 June

CHALONS

Fr Fourth
Army

NANCY

STRASBOURG

ALENÇON

Seine

ST DIZIER

Marne

EPINAL

22 June
Trapped French Third,
Fifth & Eighth Armies
surrender

RENNES

LE MANS

CHARTRES

TROYES

BELFORT

ORLÉANS

BASLE

ANGERS

Loire

TOURS

BRIARE
18 June

DIJON
16 June

PONTARLIER
17 June

SWITZERLAND

BERNE

NANTES
19 June

SAUMUR
19 June

Cher

VIERZON

NEVERS

F R A N C E

Saône

POITIERS

BAY OF BISCAY

ROYAN
25 June

ANGOULÊME

LIMOGES

CLERMONT
FERRAND

VICHY
20 June

LYONS
20 June

GENEVA

ITALY

LANSLEBOURG

TURIN

22 June 1940
Line reached by German
forces at armistice

ST ETIENNE

GRENOBLE

BRIANÇON

Italy declares
war 10 June 1940,
attacks 21 June

Rhône

BORDEAUX

Garonne

TOULOUSE

NICE

MENTON

ST JEAN DE LUZ
27 June

MARSEILLES

TOULON

PERPIGNAN

MEDITERRANEAN SEA

SPAIN

	GERMAN CONTROLLED, 4 JUNE, 1940
●●●●	WEYGAND LINE, 4 JUNE
▬·▬·▬	FRONT LINE, 11/12 JUNE

0 ————— MILES ————— 150
0 ————— KILOMETERS ————— 250

Paris on 9 June, and von Bock directed west of the capital with 50 divisions (including six panzer) four days earlier. Army Group C would attack the Maginot Line on 14 June with 24 divisions. In the event, von Bock's Fourth Army was across the Somme in a day and reached the Seine on 9 June. Elements of the French IX Corps including the British 51st Division were driven back on St Valéry-en-Caux and forced to surrender on 12 June. Von Rundstedt's forces found the going harder, but Guderian's panzer spearhead broke through the French Fourth Army at Chalons on the same day that Rommel accepted the capitulation at St Valéry. Paris was declared an open city on the following day as the Germans fanned out to the south. On 14 June Army Group C broke through the Maginot Line at Saarbrücken. Two days later Reynaud's government resigned after failing to win military support either for continuing the war from North Africa or an unlikely British proposal for an 'indissoluble union' between Britain and France. Marshal Pétain, who had been recalled from being ambassador to Madrid on 18 May, was appointed deputy Prime Minister. He assumed the reins of government on 17 June and announced that he would seek terms. On the following day de Gaulle, who had also been appointed to the government (as Under Secretary for War) but had departed for London, broadcast his intention to continue the war in the name of France. On 21 June a French delegation negotiated with Hitler in the same railway carriage at Compiégne in which a German delegation had signed the armistice in 1918. The new armistice came into effect on 25 June. A separate armistice had also been signed on the previous day with Italy. On 10 June Mussolini had seized the moment of French defeat to declare war in the expectation of easy pickings. In fact the Italian offensive which began on 20 June made little progress in southern France.

In just six weeks and at the cost of only 156,000 casualties the Germans had overrun three countries and inflicted over 391,000 casualties on the Allies, excluding the 1.9 million French troops they had captured. However, Britain was still in the war and the Blitzkrieg tactics that had proved so successful were no answer to the problems of getting across the Channel if the British declined to negotiate. Only the diminishing likelihood of Britain suing for peace brought about active consideration of an invasion (Operation Sealion) although the German Navy had tentatively considered it in November 1939. Indeed, it does not appear that Hitler seriously contemplated an invasion until 16 July 1940. The plan initially anticipated landing 13 divisions in three days – six between Ramsgate and Bexhill, four between Brighton and the Isle of Wight, and three in Lyme Bay. Subsequently this was considered impracticable and nine divisions were to be put ashore in 11 days – four between Folkestone and St Leonards, two between Bexhill and Eastbourne, and three between Beachy Head and Brighton. Two airborne divisions would also support the landing. However, neither army nor navy were optimistic about the prospects of success in the operation, which was scheduled for 21 September, and all depended upon the Luftwaffe gaining command of the skies above Britain. The latter's failure to do so led to postponement until the 27th and then on 12 October postponement until 1941.

ABOVE RIGHT: *The German victory parade through Paris.*

RIGHT: *Hitler and von Ribbentrop (rear) meet Marshal Pétain, the leader of Vichy France.*

ABOVE, FAR RIGHT: *A French medium artillery battery fights on despite the loss of the French capital.*

FAR RIGHT: *A lasting image of May 1940 – frightened refugees crowd French and Belgian roads in a futile attempt to escape the advancing Wehrmacht.*

Another danger for Britain was the possibility that the French Fleet might fall into German hands as a condition of surrender. In fact, the French had no intention of yielding their fleet, which had escaped to North Africa, but Hitler's demand that it be demobilized was regarded by Britain as essentially the same thing. Accordingly, Vice-Admiral Somerville commanding Force H at Gibraltar was ordered to secure the surrender, transfer, or destruction of French warships lying at Oran and Mers-el-Kebir. The local French naval commanders declined to comply with Somerville's requests and between 3 and 7 July four French capital ships were sunk or crippled by British naval gunfire at Oran, Mers-el-Kebir, and Dakar. Some 1297 French seamen were killed. Not unexpectedly, Operation Catapult did little for British relations with the authorities at Vichy where Pétain's government was established. Thus, when de Gaulle's newly formed Free French forces, supported by the Royal Navy, appeared off Dakar in the French West African colony of Senegal on 24 September, the Vichy garrison fought back. Rather than see Frenchmen kill their fellow countrymen de Gaulle withdrew.

In the short term, there was little that Britain could now do against Germany, but in any case attention was diverted to the implications of Italy's entry into the war. As late as 1938 British strategic plans had envisaged deploying the BEF to an 'eastern theater' – Egypt – rather than to the continent. This was a reflection not only of the importance of Middle East oil but also of the trade routes through Suez and of Britain's imperial possessions and influence in the region. In theory, the Italians posed a significant threat with a formidable number of aircraft and a fleet of five battleships, 19 cruisers, 121 destroyers or frigates, and 107 submarines. In reality, Mussolini himself had recognized Italy's underlying economic weakness when he told Hitler in May 1939 that he could not fight for three years since the country was wholly lacking in raw materials. Thus, gambling on an Allied collapse, Italy entered the war with only 1,800,000 tons of fuel oil for the fleet and only sufficient aviation fuel to last four months. Consequently, both air force and fleet remained very much on the defensive and the Italian Navy declined to be drawn out. However, even its limited operations to deny Allied access to the Tyrrhenian Sea and the Adriatic took up a million tons of the precious fuel oil, while a daring British attack on the harbor at Taranto with carrier-based aircraft on 11 November 1940 sank one Italian battleship and crippled two more.

The Italian Army was rather better placed to take action although it lacked heavy equipment. Marshal Graziani,

ABOVE: German troops on the Channel coast man a range-finder.

RIGHT: A Stuka goes into a dive against a pocket of resistance.

TOP LEFT: Hitler and his entourage arriving at Compiégne for the French surrender ceremony, 21 June 1940. Left to right: Von Brauchitsch, Raeder, Hitler, Hess, Goering, von Ribbentrop and Hitler's two adjutants, Schmundt and Brückner.

FAR LEFT: French vessels under British bombardment at Mers-el-Kebir, an action that temporarily soured Anglo-French relations.

ABOVE LEFT: Germans inspect the damage inflicted on a beached British vessel near Dunkirk.

LEFT: One of the French ships sunk by the Royal Navy at Oran.

who commanded the Italian forces in Libya, had almost 250,000 men facing only 36,000 British troops of the Western Desert Force under Major General Richard O'Connor. Similarly, the Duke of Aosta had over 290,000 troops in Italian East Africa compared to four British battalions and the Somaliland Camel Corps in neighboring British Somaliland. On 3 August 1940 Aosta advanced into British Somaliland, forcing Major General A R Godwin-Austen to evacuate his meager garrison from Berbera with naval assistance 12 days later. On 13 September Graziani also advanced into Egypt but chose to halt some 70 miles beyond the frontier to build a series of fortified camps around Sidi Barrani. O'Connor, who had conducted a skillful retirement, then launched what was intended only as a five-day raid rather than a full offensive with his 4th Indian Division – subsequently relieved by 6th Australian Division – and 7th Armored Division. But Operation Compass, which began on 8 December, threw the Italians into total disorder. The British GOC in the Middle East, General Sir Archibald Wavell, was then able to direct O'Connor to advance into Libya itself. Bardia fell almost immediately and the Australians took Tobruk on 5 January 1941. Over 38,000 Italians were surrounded in Cyrenaica and forced to capitulate on 7 February. When the British halted at El Agheila two days later, O'Connor had advanced over 500 miles and taken 130,000 prisoners, almost 400 tanks and over 1200 guns. With only two divisions at any one time, O'Connor had routed ten and suffered less than 2000 battlefield casualties.

While success attended British arms in Libya, British forces had also struck back in Somaliland. On 10 February 1941 Lieutenant General Sir Alan Cunningham launched Godwin-Austen's 12th African Division into Italian Somaliland from Kenya. Covering 275 miles in only 15 days, they took Mogadishu on 25 February after dispersing an Italian force at Jelib. Two battalions from Aden subsequently reconquered British Somaliland, taking Berbera on 16 March. Realizing that there was little opposition, Cunningham secured Wavell's consent to extend his operations into Abyssinia in an attempt to conclude the campaign before the onset of the rains in May. The 11th African Division entered Jijiga on 17 March and, despite occasional stiff Italian resistance in the mountain passes, reached Harrar on 26 March and Diredawa three days later. Aosta decided not to defend Addis Ababa and the capital was occupied on 6 April, but this still left sizeable Italian forces at large. Farther north in Eritrea, the 4th and 5th Indian Divisions under Lieutenant General Sir William

TOP: Italian troops taken by the Western Desert Force march into captivity, 16 December 1940. Wavell's small force netted over 100,000 Italians.

ABOVE: A Cruiser tank of the 1st Royal Tank Regiment on maneuvers at Abbasia in Egypt during May 1940.

RIGHT: An indication of the difficulties posed by the harsh terrain encountered during the Ethiopian campaign – 'Happy Valley' near Keren, 7 April 1941.

LEFT: The defenders of Tobruk march out on patrol during the first siege.

LEFT: The first armored cars of the Afrika Korps advance through Tripoli – a direct result of the British victory over the Italians.

BELOW LEFT: British forces move through thick scrub with bayonet fixed, Eritrea, March 1941. Italian resistance, though occasionally stubborn, was quickly overcome in East Africa.

Platt had met much stronger resistance and fighting persisted around Keren for eight weeks before the Italians withdrew south, and the garrison at Massawa on the Red Sea coast did not surrender until 8 April. An attempt to clear the Italians from the Addis Ababa to Asmara road also led to heavy fighting for a series of mountain positions before Aosta surrendered at Amba Alagi on 19 May. The rains had now begun as British forces pushed southwest toward Jimma and northwest toward Gondar. Jimma fell to the 22nd East African Brigade on 21 June, but it was not until 28 November 1941 that the remaining 22,000 Italian troops capitulated at Gondar.

Unfortunately for the British, Italian reverses prompted German intervention. On 12 January 1941, as O'Connor's offensive was still under way in Cyrenaica, a German light armored division was arriving at Tripoli under the command of General Lieutenant Erwin Rommel. At the same time, pressure was being exerted on Wavell to divert troops from the Western Desert to Greece where Italian failures would also prompt Hitler into assisting his ally. Hitler had taken advantage of a pro-German coup in Rumania in October 1940 which replaced King Carol II with a government led by General Antonescu and enabled German troops to enter the country. This had angered Mussolini, who had not been consulted, and added to his sense of frustration. He had already been prevented from obtaining French territory and colonies when Hitler declined to break up the French Empire and Italy had been excluded when Russia, Bulgaria, and Hungary had all made earlier successful bids to acquire disputed tracts of Rumanian territory. To restore Italian prestige, since he considered Rumania to lie within Italy's sphere of influence, Mussolini therefore advanced his claims on Greece. On 28 October Italian forces invaded Greece from Albania. But the 14 divisions of the Greek Army not only held against Mussolini's 28 divisions but launched a successful counterattack into Albania on 2 November and very quickly took Koritza.

Initially, the Greek dictator, General Metaxas, declined British assistance other than four squadrons of aircraft for fear of provoking German intervention but, in early January 1941, he requested ground forces. Wavell simply could not spare the nine divisions Metaxas demanded and the question of aid lapsed. But when Metaxas died suddenly at the end of January his successor made a fresh appeal. On 23 February it was agreed that 100,000 men – principally the 1st Armored Brigade Group and I Australian Corps – should be sent to Greece. The first elements left Egypt on 4 March 1941 under General Sir Henry Maitland-Wilson. Two days earlier Bulgaria had followed Hungary and Rumania into signing the Tripartite Pact with Germany and had admitted German troops. On 19 March the Germans gave the Yugoslavs five days to do likewise. The Yugoslav Regent, Prince Paul, did so on 25 March but was almost immediately overthrown in a coup led by General Simovitch. Hitler had already resolved to help Mussolini in December by attacking Greece from Bulgaria (Operation Marita) but, regarding the coup in Belgrade as a personal affront, he now ordered Yugoslavia to be attacked simultaneously with Greece. On 31 March Rommel struck in Libya and on 6 April Germany invaded Yugoslavia and Greece. The war was widening rapidly.

CHAPTER THREE

WAR ON ALL FRONTS

Panzer divisions spearheaded the German invasion of Greece and Yugoslavia on 6 April 1941. Thinly spread along their frontier with no pretense at defense in depth, the Yugoslav Army was incapable of resisting the Blitzkrieg despite its nominal strength. The bulk of the Greek Army (12 divisions) was still facing the Italians in Albania. A further four Greek divisions were holding the Metaxas Line covering Salonika in Macedonia. This left only three Greek divisions and the British forces deployed to Greece to hold the Aliakmon Line from the Aegean to the Vermion mountains. The latter risked being seriously threatened in the flank if the Germans overran Yugoslavia. Of the 100,000 men promised by the British only some 56,000 had arrived to hold what was a fortified line in name only. The 7th Australian Division was expected to follow the 6th Australian Division, New Zealand Division and British 1st Armored Brigade but could not be spared due to Rommel's offensive in Libya. The limited number of British fighter aircraft was soon overwhelmed by the Luftwaffe – one consignment of Hurricanes was lost on a cargo ship in the harbor at Piraeus on 6 April – and the Germans enjoyed total air superiority.

In Zagreb the Croats declared independence from the Serbs and welcomed the German Second Army as liberators as its troops advanced south from Austria and Hungary. Belgrade, which had been heavily bombed with the loss of 17,000 civilian lives on 6 April, fell to XLI Panzer Corps advancing from Rumania on the 12th, while the Twelfth Army swept south and west to reach the Monastir gap on the frontier between Yugoslavia and Greece. The Yugoslavs surrendered on the 17th having inflicted only 558 casualties on the Germans and marginally inconvenienced only four of the 12 German divisions committed. Meanwhile, other elements of Twelfth Army directed by Field Marshal List had broken through the Metaxas Line in just three days and Salonika had fallen to 2nd Panzer Division on 9 April. While the Greek Second Army in Thrace was compelled to surrender, Maitland-Wilson withdrew British forces toward Mount Olympus. Apart from the British 1st Armored Brigade, which suffered some loss at Kozani on 12 April, Wilson's forces had not yet been heavily engaged. However, the collapse of Yugoslavia and of the Greeks had thoroughly undermined his position. The Olympus area was untenable for defense and the British withdrew farther south to Thermopylae on 13 April.

By this time the Greek First Army had also been retiring from the Albanian front and on 16 April the Greek Commander in Chief, General Papagos, suggested that Wilson evacuate to spare further destruction of the country. The

PREVIOUS PAGES: British light tanks and infantry photographed during the invasion of Syria in June 1941.

TOP: Panzer IIIs sweep past Greek anti-tank defenses.

ABOVE: Italian troops in action in Yugoslavia during 1941.

LEFT: Greek prisoners of war march past German armored cars. The Greeks defeated early Italian thrusts, but rapidly disintegrated in the face of the Wehrmacht.

RIGHT: A column of British
artillery and mechanized
transport roll through a
Greek village – too little and
too late to influence the
outcome of the campaign.

BELOW: Italian heavy
artillery pounds Greek
positions, November 1940.

ABOVE: *German troops pour into southern Russia during the early, sweepingly successful days of* Operation Barbarossa.

LEFT: *German paratroopers drop over Heraklion airfield in Crete. One of the Ju 52s has been hit by British anti-aircraft fire.*

TOP RIGHT: *An underofficer of the Wehrmacht in Russia, June 1941.*

CENTER RIGHT: *Elite mountain troops of the German Army on their way to Crete by Junkers transport aircraft.*

RIGHT: *A German horse-drawn supply column moves through Russia in the early stages of* Barbarossa.

Surprise

Surprise is a potent psychological weapon which can cause confusion and paralysis in the enemy chain of command and destroy the cohesion and morale of his formations. It can operate at all levels. At the highest or strategic level it will invariably have a political as well as a military input. Typically, political negotiations in a time of tension might be continued until the last possible moment to confuse and deceive the victim while the attacking forces take up their positions for a decisive blow. One example of such a pre-emptive attack is that of the Japanese on Pearl Harbor in December 1941 and so too are the German offensives in the West in May 1940 and against Russia in June 1941. While often coinciding with an overall strategic plan, surprise may also be achieved at the operational level of corps or divisions as in the case of the Japanese offensive in Malaya in December 1941 while, at the tactical level, a *coup de main* such as the seizure of the Belgian fortress of Eben Emael by German glider-borne troops in May 1940 can frequently be instrumental in unhinging enemy positions as a preliminary to higher-level operations. Surprise can also operate in every phase of war, be it attack, defense, or withdrawal, although surprise in attack normally reaps the greatest dividends against a weak or badly organized foe.

The elements of surprise might be described as secrecy, concealment, deception, originality, audacity, and speed. Secrecy is an obvious requirement and was well maintained prior to the Allied invasion of Normandy in June 1944 while the British attack on the Mareth Line in

Tunisia in March 1943 was compromised by a radio transmission reminding a unit of the need to maintain radio silence. Secrecy works hand-in-hand with both concealment and deception. The Wehrmacht, for example, successfully concealed the concentration of three Panzer Corps opposite the Ardennes in 1940 and the formation of two new Panzer Armies in the very same region in December 1944. Examples of deception abound, notably in the way in which the Allies deceived the Germans as to the point at which they would invade the continent in 1944. Blitzkrieg might be regarded as an example of originality although so was the use of gliders at Eben Emael in the same campaign at a lower level. Equally, in the same campaign, the British counterattack at Arras might be seen as an example of audacity in terms of the disproportionate impact on the German High Command of a local attack by a single tank brigade. The sheer speed of the unfolding Blitzkrieg meanwhile added to Allied confusion.

However, surprise may not always work as in the case of the Allied airborne assault on Arnhem in September 1944, while accurate intelligence correctly interpreted may prevent surprise being achieved. In this regard the Allies had the enormous advantage of signals intelligence derived from ULTRA, the Poles having acquired and passed to the British in July 1939 a German Enigma coding machine which enabled the British to break the German ciphers. Nevertheless even ULTRA did not prevent the Allies being caught by the massive German attack in the Ardennes in 1944.

Greek First Army surrendered four days later and on 24 April the German 5th Panzer Division broke through the 6th Australian Division at Thermopylae. An evacuation of British forces now began and continued until the 29th. German parachutists seized the Corinth Canal bridge intact on 26 April but British officers managed to detonate the prelaid charges with revolver fire and, with sterling work by the Royal Navy, some 43,000 men were successfully taken off from Greek ports. Athens had fallen on 27 April.

Of those evacuated from Greece, about 21,000 were taken to Crete rather than Egypt since it was considered vital to hold the island for its fine natural harbor at Suda Bay. Equally, the Germans were anxious to secure Crete as a base both to guard the flank of planned operations in Russia and to deny the RAF the opportunity of operating against Rumanian oil fields. At the same time, General Kurt Student wanted to test the mettle of his German airborne forces and had devised a plan in early April to drop paratroops at seven landing zones on the island. In the event, the plan was modified to seizing only Suda Bay and the airfields at Maleme, Rhethymnon and Heráklion. Some 22,000 men were made available for Operation Mercury, of whom 10,000 from the German 7th Airborne Division would be dropped by parachute and the remainder from the 5th and 6th Mountain Divisions landed by glider or by sea. Over 1200 fighter, bomber, and transport aircraft were employed, German air superiority made it especially hazardous for British naval vessels operating north of the island.

The British were well aware of German intentions from intelligence derived from ULTRA, the British cipher-breaking operation, and Churchill welcomed the opportunity of inflicting heavy losses on Student's forces. However, although the garrison totaled 42,000 men, little had been done to prepare the defenses and many of the defenders lacked heavy equipment. Nevertheless, Major General Bernard Freyberg, the New Zealander entrusted with the defense of Crete, worked hard to improve his positions, although he was forced to send away his few remaining aircraft on 17 May. Three days later Student's paratroopers began their assault. However, they could only drop with light equipment and were dependent

TOP: *A Pzkpfw Mark III of the Afrika Korps throws up a large dust cloud as it moves at speed through the Western Desert.*

ABOVE: *German paratroopers advance against a hill-top position during the struggle for Crete during May 1941.*

LEFT: *Decorations being presented to members of the German airborne forces for their part in the capture of Crete. Their heavy losses, however, destroyed the force as a fighting unit.*

TOP RIGHT: *German machine-gunners advance through thick sand at El Brega in the Western Desert in 1941.*

CENTER RIGHT: *A German armored half-track undergoes running repairs in the heat of the North African desert.*

RIGHT: *Rommel (second right) and his staff plan a blow against the British.*

either upon landing unseen or finding weapons canisters quickly. In fact, aerial reconnaissance had been faulty and many landed directly on top of the defenders. As a result, the Germans failed to take either Rhethymnon or Heráklion but they did establish a grip on Maleme during the night of 20-21 May when, through misunderstandings, the New Zealand 5th Brigade withdrew from key positions around the airfield. Freyberg appears to have feared being outflanked by seaborne landings – one convoy of German-manned Greek *caiques* was destroyed by the Royal Navy during the night – and to have underestimated the perilous situation of the German troops. Consequently, there was only a limited counterattack toward Maleme on 22 May and, as the Germans were able to fly in reinforcements, Freyberg withdrew. Misunderstandings and lack of communications also condemned the Australian 19th Brigade at Rhethymnon to capture as other Allied forces retired on Sfakia and Heráklion. The Royal Navy had already lost heavily to German aircraft but it managed to bring out 14,967 men by 31 May. The Allied forces had lost 1800 dead, 4000 wounded and 12,000 captured. German casualties may have reached 17,000, of whom some 4000 were killed. The 7th Airborne Division in particular was a broken reed but this was small comfort to the British who had been bundled so ignominiously out of the Balkans.

The reverses came on top of Rommel's successes in Libya. Again, the British had been made aware through ULTRA of Rommel's arrival in North Africa but the need to send troops to Greece had depleted what remained of British forces in the Western Desert. Accordingly, when Rommel launched a limited raid on 31 March he found the forward British positions around El Agheila only weakly held by the 2nd Armored Division (less its brigade in Greece). General Philip Neame, VC, fell back before Rommel's advance but was unfortunate enough to lose the main British petrol dump at Msus on 3 April when it was fired by its guards on the approach of a German column. Benghazi had to be abandoned and 3rd Armored Brigade was cut off at Derna. The rest of the division fell back through Mechili to El Adem but was also surrounded and surrendered on 8 April. Neame, together with O'Connor, had been captured by a German patrol on the night of 6-7 April. The 9th Australian Division was cut off in Tobruk but held out and proved a veritable thorn in Rommel's side, for while they held the port the Germans were still forced to bring all supplies the 1000 miles from Tripoli. However, by 14 April Rommel's leading elements were at Sollum on the Egyptian frontier; their success so unsettled the German High Command that General von Paulus was sent to review the situation. Von Paulus' sanguine report on the logistic difficulties facing Rommel reached the British though ULTRA and Churchill urged Wavell to counterattack, especially as the 'Tiger' convoy had successfully carried 238 tanks through the Mediterranean to Alexandria.

Wavell had already attempted to regain control of the vital Halfaya Pass to improve the defensive position on the frontier. Led by Brigadier Gott, Operation Brevity had commenced on 15 May and achieved initial success in seizing Halfaya and Capuzzo. Unfortunately for the British, when Rommel launched a counterattack in turn, Gott promptly retired from Capuzzo. A countermanding order to prevent withdrawal arrived too late for the movement to be reversed. By 27 May Rommel was not only back on Halfaya Pass but had begun to emplace 88mm anti-aircraft guns in an anti-tank role. Thus, when Wavell renewed the offensive at Churchill's prompting in Operation Battleaxe on 15 June, the 7th Armored Brigade lost heavily. Capuzzo was taken once more and a foothold was gained on the Hafid Ridge but Rommel's 5th Light Division outflanked the British tanks around Sidi Omar on the second day and linked with 8th Panzer Division on 17 June

ABOVE: *Dead Senegalese troops of the Vichy French forces outside Saida in Syria, June 1941.*

LEFT: *Captured Vichy French equipment being repaired in British field workshops in Syria, June 1941.*

BELOW: *General Sir Claude Auchinleck, the victor of First Alamein, pictured on 31 July 1941.*

to drive the British back. The British lost 91 of the newly arrived tanks and Wavell withdrew his battered formations on the evening of 17 June. Four days later he was relieved of his command and replaced by General Sir Claude Auchinleck from India.

At least Wavell had enjoyed some success before his removal since Maitland-Wilson was by then completing the subjugation of Vichy French forces in Syria and the Lebanon. The Vichy authorities' control of these mandated territories had posed a significant threat to the British position in the Middle East and one that had grown with a pro-German coup in Iraq on 3 April. The Iraqis laid siege to the British base at Habbaniya on 2 May and forced Wavell to mount a relief operation culminating in the capture of Baghdad by Major General J G W Clark on the 31st. During the relief, however, the Vichy French in Damascus allowed German and Italian aircraft to use local airfields as bases from which to attack Habbaniya. On 8 June 20,000 British and Free French troops invaded Syria and Lebanon. It was hoped the Vichy French would not resist, but British commandos landing in Lebanon suffered heavy losses on 9 June and hard fighting followed at Kissoue and Merjuyun. Indeed, some Allied troops were surrounded and forced to surrender at Quneitra and Mezze on 16 and 19 June respectively. But Damascus fell to the Allies on 21 June after the Vichy French evacuated; Palmyra fell on 3 July and Damur on the 9th. An armistice was signed on the 14th enabling the Allies to occupy both countries. Amid the disasters the fall of Damascus was a bright spot for the Allies, but of far more significance was the opening of the German invasion of Russia on the following day. The subsequent campaign in Russia marked a turning point in the war.

Hitler's ultimate intention had always been the defeat of the Soviet Union and of communism. He had not expected to have to fight Britain and had anticipated some compromise. Now, by going ahead with the invasion of the Soviet Union he would not only fulfill his original aims

but further isolate Britain and force her eventual surrender. In any case, the division of eastern Europe following the Non-Aggression Pact was not working. The Soviets appeared to be attempting to extend their influence beyond the Baltic and to the Balkans. Stalin had ignored Hitler's suggestion in November 1940 that Russia look only toward China and Persia. As early as 21 July 1940 Hitler had directed his Commander in Chief, Field Marshal von Brauchitsch, to advise on the possibilities of beginning the attack in the fall of 1940. He had also laid down the desirability of establishing new client states in the Baltic and the Ukraine and of both defeating the Red Army and pushing back the Soviet frontier sufficiently far to secure Germany for the foreseeable future. Von Brauchitsch and his staff managed to persuade Hitler to postpone the invasion and detailed planning started on 29 July 1940 under the direction of General Marcks. The operation details of the plan took some time to finalize.

With the agreement of the German Chief of Staff, General Halder, Marcks made Moscow the main objective as the Soviet capital and a primary nodal center which the Red Army would be bound to defend. Thus, the Red Army could be defeated in detail before Moscow and the Germans could then seize as much territory as they needed. While Marcks envisaged a secondary push into the Ukraine and the exploitation of this advance once Moscow fell, 75 percent of the available armor was allocated north of the Pripet marshes. Marcks expected victory within 17 weeks. By contrast to the army staff the parallel planning of *Oberkommando der Wehrmacht* (OKW) emphasized the economic benefits of the Ukraine as well as displaying something of an obsession with the Baltic. At a major planning conference on 5 December 1940, therefore, von Brauchitsch and Halder found Hitler unconvinced by their arguments in favor of pushing straight to Moscow and 12 days later the Führer amended the operational directive prepared by OKW to make Leningrad rather than Moscow the first priority. On 18 December

BELOW: Soviet Polikarpov fighters lie shattered on the ground, destroyed in the first hours of the German onslaught against Russia.

ABOVE: Hitler and his military advisers in August 1941. From left to right: Keitel, von Brauchitsch and Halder.

LEFT: A German motorized column belonging to Guderian's command advances into Russia.

ABOVE RIGHT: A photograph later taken from the body of a German infantryman showing celebrations after the first successes of Barbarossa.

RIGHT: German armor attacks beyond the River Dniepr, July 1941.

Hitler signed Directive No 21 ordering commencement of Operation *Barbarossa* in May 1941.

Hitler's subsequent decision in March 1941 to invade Greece and Yugoslavia played a part in delaying *Barbarossa*. A month's postponement was ordered in March although only 29 out of the 152 divisions written into the *Barbarossa* plan were diverted to the Balkans. Only three divisions then remained in Greece after the Allied withdrawal and 11 were placed in OKH Reserve so that only 15 were required to redeploy. The Germans could have begun *Barbarossa* earlier therefore, although the use of VIII Air Corps in the battle for Crete was an additional difficulty. Nevertheless, the delay in starting the operations against the Soviets – the date for which (22 June) was finally set by Hitler on 29 May – owed rather more to German confidence in being able to defeat the Red Army than to the help given Mussolini in the Balkans. Both the Finns and the Rumanians, whose participation Hitler had enlisted, had also required more time to prepare, and the late thaw in the spring of 1941 was another factor.

The final plan gave 29 divisions to Field Marshal von Leeb's Army Group North tasked with the advance on Leningrad; 50 to Field Marshal von Bock's Army Group Center, which would encircle and destroy the Red Army in Belorussia and then co-operate with von Leeb to ensure the fall of Leningrad before possibly pushing for Moscow; and 42 to Field Marshal von Rundstedt's Army Group South to drive into the Ukraine. The Finns would help in isolating Leningrad and the Rumanians would support the advance into the Ukraine. With reserves, 153 German, 18 Finnish and 12 Rumanian divisions were deployed with over 3.5 million men and 3500 tanks. The Red Army had 360 divisions in the west rather than the 225 the Germans anticipated and the whole enterprise was really a colossal gamble. The capture of Czech, Polish, and French mate-

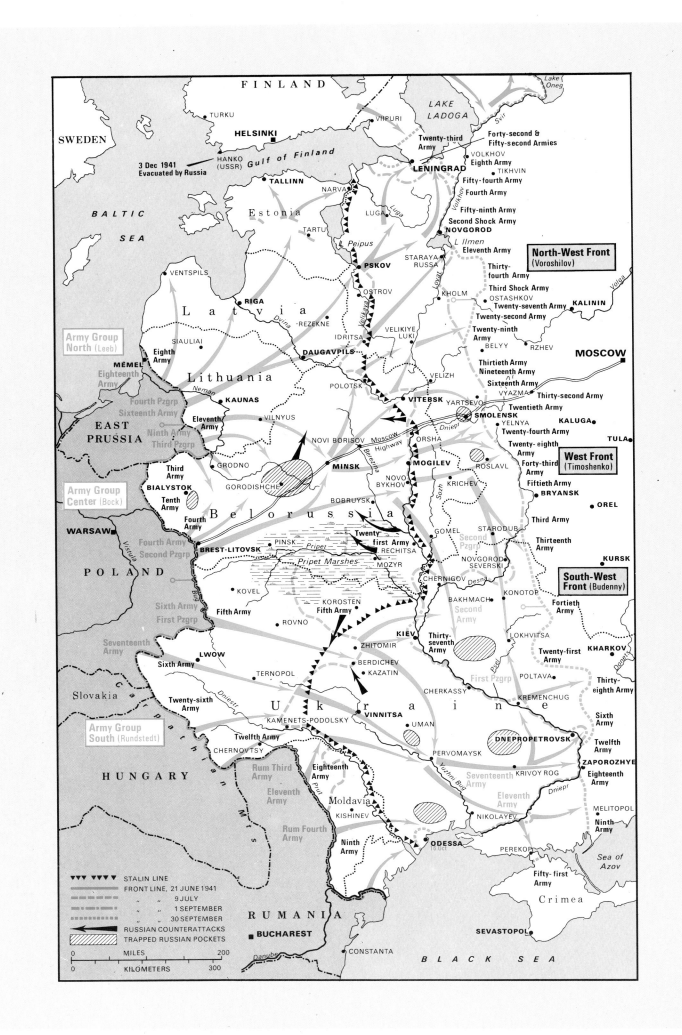

ABOVE: Luftwaffe Stukas are prepared for another mission in Russia.

RIGHT: A German 37mm anti-tank gun destroys an armored vehicle during the advance in southern Russia.

ABOVE: The opening phase of Operation Barbarossa.

riel had not sufficed to make good the transport deficiencies in the German Army. There were but 15 motorized and 19 panzer divisions in the order of battle and the majority of the 119 infantry divisions could advance only as fast as they could march. Within just 19 days a third of the lorry transport would have broken down and the Germans reduced to relying on horsed transport. Yet the opening stages of Barbarossa were a spec-

tacular success. The Soviets had good intelligence of German preparations both from British warnings and their own spies, but Stalin failed to alert his armies and surprise was complete when the German artillery and air bombardment opened up at 0300 on 22 June. Surprise allowed the Germans to make deep advances.

With two panzer groups assigned, von Bock's Army Group Center advanced toward Minsk. Hoth's 3rd Panzer

Group and Guderian's 2nd Panzer Group had originally been ordered to close pincers on Smolensk but Hitler had vetoed this as too risky. In the event, when they linked up at Minsk on 27 June they had surrounded the whole of the Soviet Third and Tenth Armies as well as elements of three others and they had netted 290,000 prisoners. As the Red Army collapsed under the onslaught, Stalin sent Timoshenko, the man responsible for rebuilding the armies after the Finnish debacle, to restore order as Guderian and Hoth moved on Smolensk. Timoshenko's predecessor was summarily executed but the newcomer could do little more and Guderian and Hoth cut off the Sixteenth and Twentieth Armies west of the city. Another 300,000 prisoners had fallen into German hands by the time the Smolensk pocket was cleared on 5 August. To the north, von Leeb's advance was hampered by his own disagreements with General Hoepner commanding the 4th Panzer Group but he was still well into Estonia by mid-July. In the south, von Rundstedt's 1st Panzer Group, commanded by General von Kleist, also advanced rapidly and surrounded 103,000 men of the Soviet Sixth and Twelfth Armies around Uman on 2 August.

Halder now wanted Guderian and Hoth to attempt a third encirclement in front of Moscow and to concentrate all resources for a drive on the capital. But Hitler, who had been starting to interfere in detailed operational planning,

now proposed to divert Hoth to the north and Guderian to the south. On 30 July he was persuaded to cancel the directives he had issued for these operations but Army Group Center was still halted. Halder made a number of attempts to get the advance on Moscow restarted but on 20 August Hitler ruled that Leningrad and the Ukraine were more important objectives. Guderian was sent south and linked with von Kleist at Lokhvitsa on 16 September in yet another vast encirclement that trapped the Soviet Fifth, Twenty-first, Twenty-sixth and Thirty-seventh Armies around Kiev. Some 665,000 more prisoners were taken. Von Leeb had meanwhile come within sight of Leningrad on 10 September and cut the land route into the city but the Finns declined to advance farther south than the Svir and von Leeb could only begin a blockade.

The early capture of Moscow would not necessarily have ended the war and Hitler was essentially correct in recognizing the economic importance of the Ukraine to both Germany and the Soviet Union. But his precise thinking was never clear, and somewhat illogically he changed his mind and supported a resumed drive on Moscow. Von Leeb and von Rundstedt were now stripped of seven panzer divisions for Operation Typhoon, with 3rd and 4th Panzer Groups ordered to execute another pincer movement on Vyazma some 80 miles behind the Soviet front at Smolensk while Guderian advanced northeast from Glukhov toward Moscow. Not expecting the sudden switch in direction, the Soviets were again caught by surprise as Guderian started his attack on 30 September. The German Second Army advancing alongside Guderian bagged 50,000 prisoners in the Bryansk pocket between 3 and 25 October but this effort was too far south to make much difference to the success or otherwise of the main assault on Moscow. This began on 2 October with Hoepner's 4th Panzer Group and the 3rd, now commanded by General Reinhardt, encircling Vyazma by 7 October to yield another 650,000 prisoners. However, on that same day,

the weather broke. There was undoubted panic in Moscow as the German advance continued but the Wehrmacht was increasingly hampered by mud, the heavy wear and tear on vehicles, and the sheer exhaustion of the sustained effort since June. The turn in the weather also wreaked havoc on the Russian railways which the Germans were endeavoring to press into service. Yet despite the logistic problems, both Hitler and his generals concurred in continuing operations. The 3rd and 4th Panzer Groups were launched on an attempt to encircle Moscow itself in mid-November, Hoepner coming within 25 miles of the city. But on 6 December there was a counterattack by Marshal Zhukov, who had been placed in command of the Soviet West Front on 9 October after distinguishing himself at Leningrad.

Hitler forbade withdrawal but in places the Wehrmacht was forced back up to 200 miles. Retribution followed. In the south, von Rundstedt had pushed deep into the Ukraine with von Manstein's Eleventh Army taking 100,000 prisoners in the Crimea. Odessa had been taken by the Rumanians on 16 October and the Germans took Kharkov on the 25th, Kursk on 2 November and Rostov on the Don on the 20th. But this had created an exposed salient and von Rundstedt ordered a retirement from Rostov. On 30 November he was sacked. For ordering similar tactical withdrawals, Guderian was dismissed on 26 December and Hoepner on 8 January 1942. In all, 33 German generals were removed in December or January including both von Leeb and von Bock. Hitler also sacked von Brauchitsch and assumed the role of Commander in Chief himself on 19 December. An even more momentous decision had been to declare war on the United States on 11 December following Japan's attack on Pearl Harbor four days earlier.

President Roosevelt, who had been re-elected president for a second term in November 1940, had been edging ever closer to a commitment to Britain and its Allies.

He was well aware that he might not yet carry a majority of American opinion with him but in some respects he had already abandoned neutrality. In September 1940 Roosevelt had agreed to loan the British 50 old destroyers in return for long-term leases on British naval bases in the Caribbean. These were finally delivered in April 1941 following passage of the Lend Lease Act on 11 March. Churchill had also got Roosevelt's agreement to American warships escorting convoys in the western Atlantic – a clear breach of neutrality. German U-boats had fired torpedoes at US Navy destroyers in September and October 1941 and the USS *Reuben Jones* was sunk, although the Americans did not retaliate. Roosevelt had spoken in ringing terms of the United States being an arsenal of democracy in December 1940 and between 9 and 12 August 1941 he had met with Churchill off Newfoundland to sign the Atlantic Charter. a statement of fundamental principles to define the post-war world. Nevertheless, Hitler's declaration of war upon the United States was undoubtedly convenient for Roosevelt. It was also most timely for the British and the Soviets and immeasurably increased the potential of the wartime Alliance against Hitler. The first fruits of Anglo-Soviet co-operation had already been demonstrated by the military partition of Persia between 24 August and 17 September 1941 to prevent German influence prevailing there.

At the same time as Japan attacked the United States, it had also launched an offensive against the British in the Far East; Malaya was invaded on 8 December 1941. However, the Japanese had signed a neutrality pact with Stalin on 13 April 1941 and there were to be no hostilities between Moscow and Tokyo until August 1945. Essentially, the Japanese quarrel was with the United States although Britain had also shared American anxiety at the extent of Japanese ambitions in the Far East. Having invaded Manchuria in 1931, the Japanese had then extended their operations to the remainder of China in 1937. When they

General Winter

There is little doubt of the importance of Russia's traditional ally – 'General Winter' – in the halting of the German offensive toward Moscow in December 1941. Army Group Center experienced a drop in temperature down to -15 deg. C with the first winter frost on the night of 12 November 1941 and -20 deg. C on the following night. By December temperatures were between -30 and -40 deg. C. In all, over 100,000 cases of frostbite occurred among the Wehrmacht soldiers during the winter of 1941-2, (frostbite could occur at a temperature of only -1 deg. C). However, the difficulties encountered were not so much due to the oft-quoted absence of winter clothing than to the effect of the cold weather on the logistic system, which had been breaking down rapidly even before the onset of rains in October. If anything the first frosts made movement of wheeled vehicles easier than in the mud of October and early November, but it paralyzed the railways on which the system depended and equipment could not be brought forward quickly enough. Nevertheless, fuel oil would freeze at temperatures of -20 deg. C or below and this obviously affected motor vehicles, engines having to be run for at least 15 minutes in every two hours in order to ensure they did not seize up.

Soviet troops advance to relieve Leningrad.

ABOVE: German troops, wrapped up to combat the Russian winter, move through a village.

LEFT: The arrival of mail from home on the Eastern Front. Regular letters helped maintain morale at a time when the lack of warm clothing was a serious threat to the men's fighting spirit.

occupied the southern part of French Indochina on 24 July 1941, both Britain and the United States froze Japanese assets. But above all it was Roosevelt's imposition of an oil embargo which threatened the Japanese since nine-tenths of her oil was imported. Negotiations between the United States and Japan continued until 26 November, the Americans being greatly assisted by their ability to read Japanese diplomatic codes. But the Japanese had already decided upon war. There was no collusion with the Germans or Italians with whom Japan had entered a Tripartite Pact on 27 September 1940. Hitler had not bothered to inform the Japanese of his plans to invade Russia and the Japanese did not reveal their plans to strike at Pearl Harbor.

In seeking to obtain quick victories and a defendable perimeter from which to negotiate with the Americans, the Japanese could not afford to alert either the United

ABOVE: Sharing a cigarette and a joke during a quiet moment on the Eastern Front.

RIGHT: The Japanese attack on Pearl Harbor. The attack was well executed but failed to knock out the US Navy's carrier force.

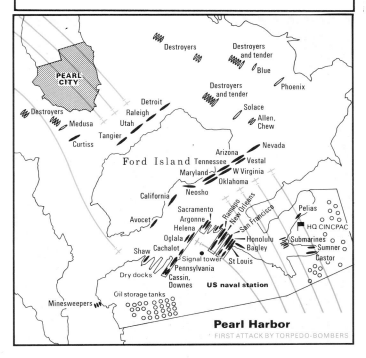

Pearl Harbor

FIRST ATTACK BY TORPEDO-BOMBERS

The Special Relationship

The warmth of the personal relationship between Winston Churchill and Franklin D Roosevelt should not disguise the fact that there were to be fundamental dis-agreements between Britain and the United States during the war. The Americans wanted to end the war against Germany quickly in order to concentrate against Japan. Therefore, they favored a cross-Channel invasion of northwest Europe at an early stage rather than any exploitation of indirect warfare in the Middle East and Mediterranean. The British commitment to the latter was strong, both because of its importance as a British sphere of influence, and also because it was an area in which Britain could carry out offensive operations from its own resources. The United States re-luctantly endorsed operations in the Mediterranean at the Casablanca Confe-rence in January 1943 but demanded an early commitment to fighting a campaign in northwest Europe at both the Washing-ton Trident Conference in May 1943 and the Quebec Quadrant Conference in August. The British then won a postpone-ment of the invasion at the Tehran and Cairo Conferences in November 1943 in view of Allied success in Italy but had to agree to release troops for a landing in the south of France. The Americans stead-fastly refused to budge from this position and declined to allow any subsequent advance to capture Vienna through the Ljubljana Gap. Similarly, they vetoed any attempt to reach Berlin before the Russians. In fact, both British proposals were unsound on logistic grounds. If the British proved obstinate then the Americans could and did play the Pacific card to full effect.

ABOVE: *Japanese Mitsubishi Zero fighters wait for the signal to take off on the Pearl Harbor mission.*

BELOW: *Anti-aircraft fire bursting over Pearl Harbor mingles with the smoke and debris rising from 'Battleship Row,' 7 December 1941.*

understandings and failings in communications, command and intelligence in both Washington and Hawaii resulted in the Japanese achieving total surprise.

The aircraft of the first wave hit Pearl Harbor and US airfields at 0755 on Sunday 7 December – the 'day of infamy' in Roosevelt's words. Seven of the eight US battleships in port were severely damaged, the *Arizona* and *Oklahoma* both capsized. Military and civilian casualties ran to 3581 of whom 2403 were killed. It was a less devastating blow than at first appeared since the American aircraft carriers so vital to the Allied war effort in the Pacific were fortuitously absent. However, for the time being, the United States could not match the strength of the Japanese carrier force. The loss of the British capital ships HMS *Repulse* and HMS *Prince of Wales* to Japanese aircraft on 10 December when they were operating without air support off Malaya struck a further blow at Allied naval power in the Pacific.

Just as Yamamoto had faced opposition in his plans to strike at Pearl Harbor, there had been a vigorous debate within the Japanese High Command on the strategic plan to be executed at the outbreak of war. The compromise adopted in August 1941 envisaged any attack on Pearl Harbor coinciding with the seizure of Thailand and assaults on Malaya, Hong Kong, the Philippines, the Gilberts, Guam, and Wake. Subsequently, it was intended to take Singapore, the Dutch East Indies, and southern Burma before consolidating control over the Dutch islands and the remainder of Burma. Since the war in China was still regarded by the Japanese Army as its first priority, only 11 divisions were available for other operations. Three were assigned to General Yamashita's Twenty-fifth Army for Malaya and Singapore; two to General Homma's Fourteenth Army for the Philippines; two to General Iida's Fifteenth Army for Burma and two to General Imamura's Sixteenth Army for the Dutch East Indies.

States or Britain by seizing the oil fields of the Dutch East Indies first. Consequently, they resolved to strike both powers simultaneously. The key to success would be to neutralize the US Pacific Fleet at Pearl Harbor in Hawaii. Admiral Yamamoto, Commander in Chief of the Combined Fleet, devised a plan to use six of the Imperial Navy's ten aircraft carriers to launch a surprise attack. This finally won acceptance in early November 1941. Leaving an isolated anchorage in the Kuriles on 26 November, the strike force headed east under the command of Vice-Admiral Nagumo. It went undetected despite American awareness of the likelihood of war, and a series of mis-

ABOVE: President Roosevelt signs the declaration of war on Japan, 11 December 1941.

RIGHT: The destroyer USS Cassin *leans on the USS* Downes *in Pearl Harbor's dry dock; the battleship USS* Pennsylvania *is in the background.*

BELOW: 'Battleship Row' *after the Japanese attack, with (left to right) the USS* Maryland, *the capsized USS* Oklahoma, *the sinking USS* West Virginia *and the USS* Tennessee.

Despite spirited resistance Wake, Guam, and Hong Kong had all been overwhelmed by the end of December. In Malaya, the situation of the British and Imperial troops deteriorated rapidly despite the fact that the defenders mustered 85,000 men compared to the 60,000 Japanese committed. But British formations were not concentrated and had anticipated an advance into Thailand in response to any Japanese threat. In any case, they were little prepared for waging a campaign in the jungle terrain of the peninsula and would have to do so without adequate air support. The Indian 11th Division fared especially badly as it retreated southward although it did hold its positions around Kampar between 27 December and 3 January 1942 and enabled the Indian 9th Division to avoid being cut off in the east. Wavell, who had replaced Auchinleck as Commander in Chief in India, was now appointed Supreme Commander of Allied Forces in the Southwest Pacific. He ordered Lieutenant General Percival to pull back to Johore where a stand might be made with the newly arrived Australian 8th Division and British 18th Division. However, continuing lack of resolution forced Percival back into Singapore island. A failure to concentrate the defenders sufficiently helped the Japanese get across the Straits of Johore on the night of 8 February. Losing control of the water supplies, Percival surrendered on 15 February 1942 with over 70,000 men, some of whom had not even fired a shot. In all, Allied casualties in the Malayan campaign were 9000 dead and wounded and 130,000 captured: the Japanese casualties were some 9800.

While the Japanese were landing in Malaya, Japanese aircraft were launching sustained attacks on American airfields in the Philippines which destroyed the US Far East Air Force. Outlying islands in the Philippines archipelago were easily overrun, but it was not until 20 December that the main invasion began with 43,000 men of Homma's army landing in Luzon's Lingayen Gulf to be followed by a further 7000 at Lamon Bay two days later. The Commander in Chief of United States Forces Far East, Lieutenant General Douglas MacArthur, had only one regular US Army division but still aimed to offer an active defense. But it soon became clear that there was little hope of holding the Japanese and on 23 December MacArthur began falling back on the Bataan peninsula and the forts in Manila Bay. Not without difficulties, the attackers were held up in Bataan by 6 January but supplies were low and the defenders were plagued by disease. On 23 February Roosevelt ordered MacArthur to leave for Australia, the general making his celebrated remark, 'I shall return,' when touching down there on 17 March.

The Japanese broke through the defense lines on Bataan between 3 and 7 April and forced the capitulation of Major General King's I Corps two days later. Some 600 Americans and between 5000 and 10,000 Filipinos died on the notorious 'Death March' from Bataan to Camp O'Donnell as 78,000 troops passed into captivity. On 5 May Lieutenant General Wainwright surrendered the battered offshore island of Corregidor, 1000 Japanese having been sufficient to neutralize a garrison of 15,000 though many of the latter were base details. To spare his men from Japanese excesses, Wainwright also surrendered the rest of the Philippines. The Dutch East Indies had gone the same way by 8 March following the dispersal of Rear Admiral Doorman's *ad hoc* Combined Striking Force of five cruisers and nine destroyers in the Battle of the Java Sea on 27 February.

In Burma, Iida's Fifteenth Army had taken Moulmein by 30 January and forced the British back to the Sittang river. The Indian 17th Division found itself heavily engaged and on 23 February the Sittang bridge was destroyed with two brigades still on the wrong side of the river. Wavell sacked Lieutenant General Hutton, who was replaced by General the Honorable Sir Harold Alexander. But Alexander, too,

soon decided that Hutton had been correct to doubt the efficacy of defending Rangoon. Accordingly, it was abandoned and fell to the Japanese on 9 March. With Lieutenant General William Slim now commanding a reorganized Burma Corps, the British conducted an epic 1000-mile fighting retreat – the longest in the British Army's history – back across the Irrawaddy and the Chindwin rivers. The Chinese Fifth and Sixth Armies were also driven back and the Japanese overran the terminal of the Burma Road linking to China at Lashio on 29 April. By 20 May 1942 all Burma was in Japanese hands.

ABOVE: *Japanese troops celebrate another runaway victory.*

TOP LEFT: *Advancing Japanese troops move through a Malayan rubber plantation, December 1941.*

CENTER LEFT: *Lieutenant General Yamashita receives the surrender of Singapore, 15 February 1942.*

ABOVE RIGHT: *Japanese forces lower the US flag over Corregidor after its surrender, 6 May 1942.*

LEFT: *Some of the thousands of Allied prisoners taken after the fall of Singapore.*

RIGHT: *Japanese troops pause outside a Buddhist temple in Burma during the rapid conquest of the peninsula.*

FAR RIGHT: *Douglas MacArthur with his chief of staff, Lieutenant General Sutherland, outside the Malinta tunnel on Corregidor.*

CHAPTER FOUR

THE ALLIES STRIKE BACK

Almost as soon as he had taken up command in the Middle East, Auchinleck found Churchill pressing him to renew the offensive against Rommel. But Auchinleck declined to do so before November 1941 and took the opportunity to rebuild and reorganize the British forces. A new British Eighth Army was created under the command of the victor of East Africa, Cunningham. In turn, Cunningham divided his command into two corps – XIII, which was predominately infantry; and XXX Corps, which was mostly armored. While innovatory in departing from the former practice of dispersing tanks among the infantry, the new organization created neither an all-armor striking force as had been advocated by many pre-war armored theorists nor an all-arms formation along German lines. Cunningham had 453 tanks in XXX Corps which matched the 412 German and Italian tanks at Rommel's disposal, but in reality the British Mark Is or 'Matildas' were seriously undergunned compared to the tanks of Rommel's 15th and 21st Panzer Divisions.

Seeking to envelop Rommel's right flank with his armor, Cunningham finally launched his offensive – Operation Crusader – on 18 November 1941. As planned, XXX Corps established itself on high ground at Sidi Rezergh while XIII Corps contained the German defenses between Sidi Omar and the sea and the Tobruk garrison sallied out in the enemy rear. However, the threat to Sidi Rezergh was quickly grasped by the commander of the German armor, General Cruewell, and by Rommel. On 20 November Rommel ordered his panzers to strike through the rear of XXX Corps, and a highly confusing tank battle ensued which lasted for two weeks. Alarmed at the loss of tanks, Cunningham requested permission to break off the battle only to be removed by Auchinleck on 26 November and replaced with Major General Ritchie. Tobruk was briefly relieved on 28 November before German efforts closed the ring once more but Rommel was also suffering losses and

on 7 December he began to extricate his command, retiring across Cyrenaica to El Agheila. Rommel had lost 300 tanks and the British 278.

Expected British reinforcements were now diverted to the Far East to meet the Japanese threat to Singapore and India. Moreover, Auchinleck also lost three divisions and 7th Armored Brigade for the same reason. Rommel, meanwhile, did get fresh supplies across the Mediterranean and on 21 January 1942 he struck once more and forced Ritchie's now over-extended army back to Gazala west of Tobruk by 4 February. Both sides continued to rebuild. Churchill was still urging Auchinleck into action since ULTRA was enabling the British to intercept many of Rommel's seaborne convoys and gave London a ready appreciation of his actual strength. Rommel himself had resolved to attack before Auchinleck did so and launched a new offensive on the Gazala line on 26 May.

Although aware that an attack was pending, the British were still surprised as Rommel's tanks swept around the southern end of the British line – the Free French 'box' at Bir Hacheim. Auchinleck had urged Ritchie to keep his armor massed in the north for counterattacks but the latter had not done so and British tanks were committed piecemeal. Two hundred were lost in brigade-sized attacks on a German defensive laager near 'Knightsbridge' into which Rommel consolidated his armor. To the south the Free Frenchmen fought a desperate battle before cutting their way out of Bir Hacheim on 10 June. Two days later Ritchie had barely 60 tanks left and had to retreat. Churchill insisted that Tobruk be held at all costs despite a previously agreed policy of avoiding another siege, while Auchinleck favored trying to hold a line of which Tobruk was merely part. In fact the line had already given way and 33,000 men – primarily the South African 2nd Infantry Brigade – were bottled up in Tobruk with little organization and virtually no defense lines remaining

PREVIOUS PAGES: Australian troops blast away with a 6-pounder anti-tank gun in the Western Desert, July 1942. The 6-pounder was capable of penetrating the armor of most German tanks in the desert.

RIGHT: A Pzkpfw Mark III of the Afrika Korps drives by one of its victims.

BELOW RIGHT: German prisoners march into captivity under British escort, 26 November 1941.

BELOW: An Afrika Korps armored column heads up to the front.

from the previous siege. On 18 June the German investment was complete and two days later Stukas and artillery smashed a way through the minefields for the infantry and tanks. The garrison surrendered next morning. XIII Corps tried to stop Rommel at Mersa Matruh on 25 June and that same day Auchinleck relieved Ritchie and assumed command of Eighth Army in person.

The retreat finally ended on a 40-mile line between El Alamein on the coast and the Qattara Depression. It was only thinly held but Rommel had also exhausted his resources in the headlong advance from Gazala. Indeed, the Germans had only 85 tanks left. Auchinleck made use of the time to reorganize into battlegroups, thinning down the immobile infantry in defensive boxes and creating mobile reserves of lorry-borne infantry with 25-pounder guns. He also concentrated the rest of the artillery under central control. Auchinleck anticipated Rommel's plan to drive through the British center and sweep north and south, and planned to counter it by striking at the German flanks with the battlegroups and the remnants of 1st Armored Division, and by these means Rommel's attempted breakthrough on 1 July was absorbed. However, Auchinleck's counterattacks did not make the headway hoped for between 2 and 5 July and a see-sawing battle continued until the 27th, although Rommel himself recognized that his forces had been effectively beaten ten days before the battle ended. This First Battle of Alamein was a tremendous tactical success for Auchinleck but he could not exploit it and proposed halting operations until September. Churchill was not satisfied and, after visiting the Middle East in person, sacked Auchinleck on 8 August. Churchill had intended to appoint Gott to command Eighth Army with Alexander as Commander in Chief in Cairo but Gott had been killed when an airplane carrying him was shot down on 7 August and he was replaced by Lieutenant General Bernard Montgomery.

ULTRA was still providing details of Rommel's logistic plight and it had also revealed his operational plans for yet another 'right hook.' Circling around the southern end of the British positions, Rommel now intended to strike toward the Alam Halfa ridge. Auchinleck had made preparations for such a contingency, aiming to create the reality of an all-arms response by combining artillery, armor, and lorry-borne infantry in a counterstroke from defended positions on the ridge. These plans were adopted by Montgomery though he subsequently chose to conceal his debt to Auchinleck. Montgomery also now had 767 tanks against Rommel's 200, complete air superiority, and ample supplies of fuel denied Rommel. On 30

TOP LEFT: Two members of a German flak artillery battery pose by an abandoned British Matilda tank and the grave of one of its crew, 29 April 1942.

CENTER LEFT: Tobruk's harbor, littered with supply ships after its capture by the Germans in June 1942.

LEFT: An Afrika Korps Pzkpfw Mark IV with a short-barreled 75mm gun. Its crew ride on the superstructure to avoid the stifling heat of the interior.

ABOVE: *A German towed 88mm anti-tank gun in the desert, July 1942.*

RIGHT: *German troops move toward the British positions around Alamein.*

BELOW: *British troops thread their way past abandoned Valentine tanks. Slow moving and undergunned, the Valentine was highly vulnerable to anti-tank fire in the open wastes of the Western Desert.*

August the German advance was held up by defensive minefields, air attack, and the desperate shortage of fuel for the German tanks. By 2 September Rommel was forced to abandon the advance, having lost 50 tanks.

Montgomery was not yet ready to advance and spent September and October accepting new tanks and reinforcements and working at his personal style of leadership. By the time his offensive – the Second Battle of Alamein – began on 23 October he had 1029 tanks including 170 Grants and 252 Shermans compared to Rommel's 489 Mark IIIs and Mark IVs. He also had 2311 guns to Rommel's 1219 and 750 aircraft to Rommel's 350 serviceable machines. The supply shortage and Rommel's own absence on sick leave in Germany was also known. The *Afrika Korps* had laid a defensive minefield four miles in depth along the whole 40-mile front and the first task was to clear paths through this barrier under cover of an opening barrage. The bombardment began at 2130 on 22 October. XXX Corps would open two corridors to a line designated as 'Oxalic' for 1st and 10th Armored Divisions but the British armor would wait for German counterattacks while the infantry 'crumbled' the opposing defenses. XIII Corps would launch diversionary attacks to draw off German armor to the south. The British tanks were delayed by congestion in the cleared corridors and were still not clear by 24 October, but Rommel's absence and the death of his temporary replacement General Stumme from heart failure ensured a surprisingly weak German response.

Rommel had returned by 26 October and more determined German attacks compelled Montgomery to regroup and switch the emphasis of attack to the northernmost corridor with 7th Armored Division pulled out of

RIGHT: British 25-pounders, silhouetted against their own gun flashes, bombard German positions during the opening phase of Second Alamein, October 1942.

BELOW RIGHT: A British sentry stands over a wounded German officer. For the infantry, Second Alamein was a bloody close-quarters battle.

BOTTOM RIGHT: Afrika Korps officers direct the fire of the feared 88mm anti-aircraft gun against ground targets.

Logistics

It is not often appreciated just how far military movements depend upon getting logistics right. In earlier ages an army might require few resources in order to function. Both men and animals could conceivably live off the land through which an army passed while the quantity of ammunition fired in the course of a campaign was usually surprisingly small. However, such logistic requirements steadily increased with the greater size, greater technological complexity, and more sophisticated diets of modern armies. During World War I, for example, an average American infantryman consumed some 40 to 50lbs of supplies of all kinds every day but his World War II counterpart was calculated as requiring 66.8lbs of supplies a day in the European theater and 67.4lbs a day in the Pacific theater. A US infantry division of 40,000 men required 1600 tons of supplies of all kinds every day and while in the field consumed 68,500 gallons of fuel per 100 miles traveled. An armored division would require 146,000 gallons per 100 miles traveled while the demand for petroleum-related products and lubricants (POL) increased enormously.

Quite staggering quantities of supplies would be needed for individual operations – the invasion of Okinawa in the Pacific in April 1945 required 747,100 tons of supplies conveyed in 430 ships. Moreover, the strategy of the war itself might turn on logistics. The Wehrmacht's lack of logistic support finally told against it in Russia in

1941 since the earlier Blitzkrieg campaigns had been won before such difficulties became too apparent. The British campaign in Burma was a struggle waged as much against logistic problems as the Japanese. Allied grand strategy was also bedeviled by a shortage of landing craft which led to agonizing debates on the priorities to be accorded to operations in northwest Europe, the Mediterranean and the Pacific.

Another classic example of the dominating role of logistics is Rommel's efforts in the Western Desert. The desert provided no food, fuel, ammunition, or spare parts and everything required had to be transported from Europe to Tripoli, which was the only satisfactory port on the North African coast. But once there the supplies still had to be transported to the front which, at the height of the Afrika Korps' success, was 1000 miles distant. Transport would therefore have to complete a 2000-mile round trip and at least 35 percent was constantly out of repair. In the process at least ten percent of the fuel landed would have been lost just transporting the remainder but fuel was by no means the only requirement at the front and between 30 and 50 percent of all fuel was probably lost in this way. It is therefore hardly surprising that Rommel was constantly short of supplies however efficient the Germans or Italians were in getting them to Tripoli. The position could only deteriorate as the German lines of communication came under air attack.

XIII Corps to come north. The Australian 9th Division made further attacks in the north on 28 October to force Rommel to commit more reserves there and on 2 November 151st and 152nd Infantry Brigades with 9th Armored Brigade commenced 'Supercharge' to effect a breakout north of Kidney Hill. Although the 9th Armored Brigade suffered heavy losses, 1st and 10th Armored Divisions were able to exploit the breakthrough on 4 November. With only 90 serviceable tanks when Montgomery still had over 600, Rommel had resolved to retreat on 2 November. His request to Berlin to do so was intercepted by ULTRA. British casualties amounted to 13,500 while Rommel had at least 7800 dead and wounded and 24,000 men, most Italian, captured.

Ever cautious, Montgomery did not follow up immediately. In any case, the armor which had been supposed to constitute a new X Corps for pursuit had suffered so heavily that 7th Armored Division and the New Zealand

ABOVE RIGHT: British Sherman tanks, armed with 75mm guns, at Alamein. Montgomery's armored force was more than double the strength of Rommel's during the battle.

RIGHT: A German Pzkpfw Mark III 'Special' at a desert halt. Spaced frontal armor improved its battlefield performance.

ABOVE: *American troops manhandle artillery ashore during the Torch landings in North Africa during November 1942.*

LEFT: *British Crusader and Sherman tanks entering Mersa Matruh in pursuit of the Afrika Korps after the Battle of Alamein.*

RIGHT: *A German 88mm anti-aircraft gun attempts to slow the British advance toward Tunisia after Alamein. The gun's high profile made it difficult to conceal on a battlefield.*

Division had to be substituted under X Corps command for 1st and 10th Armored Divisions. Rommel conducted a masterful withdrawal, and 21st Panzer Division (a panzer division in name only) escaped encirclement at Mersa Matruh on 7 May. Tobruk was recaptured by the British on 13 November and Benghazi on 20 November as Rommel fell back once more on El Agheila. Here Rommel was able to halt for three weeks, but he now had only 30 tanks while Montgomery built up laboriously for another set-piece attack. Rommel slipped away on 12 December, the night before Montgomery's planned attack. Hitler demanded a stand at Buerat and Rommel attempted to do so on 15 January 1943 but was forced to retreat once more. Tripoli fell to the British eight days later and by 12 February Rommel had been pushed back into Tunisia.

As the Afrika Korps withdrew the Allies struck behind them. As early as October 1941 Churchill had proposed a seaborne landing in North Africa. Once the United States had entered the war, he got Roosevelt's agreement at the Arcadia Conference in Washington in December 1941 to provide US troops and shipping for the invasion. Operation Torch was initially supposed to coincide with Auchinleck's advance but this had soon stalled. Nevertheless, Torch would have the advantage of bringing early American commitment to the European theater, speeding the defeat of Rommel and opening up the Mediterranean to Allied shipping. The disadvantage was the need to convince the Vichy French authorities in North Africa that they should co-operate and the operation was purposely represented as an entirely American one. Lieutenant General Dwight D Eisenhower was therefore appointed to command Torch with another American, Major General Mark W Clark, as his deputy.

The real objectives of Torch were Bizerta and Tunis but it was decided to go ashore at Casablanca, Oran, and Algiers so as to be out of reach of Axis airplanes in Sicily and Sardinia but close enough to Spanish Morocco to deal with the Spaniards if they suddenly joined the Axis. Following abortive negotiations with the Vichy French, the

operation began on 8 November 1942. There were mixed responses from the French forces in Algeria and Morocco and, by the time the Vichy authorities had decided to co-operate, valuable days had been lost. Paratroopers of British First Army took Bône on 12 November but the Germans had already reacted by flying reinforcements into Tunis. On 27 November the Germans also occupied the Vichy zone of France and tried to seize the French Fleet at Toulon, only for it to be scuttled before they could reach the harbor.

BELOW: A British Grant tank ploughs through a muddy stretch of road during the pursuit of Rommel in November 1942. Poor weather and several command errors allowed Rommel to fight another day.

RIGHT: Lieutenant General George S Patton (in the front of the scout car) directing the advance on Gabes in Tunisia by his US II Corps, March 1943.

BELOW: Soldiers of the 2nd Battalion, US 16th Infantry, march through Kasserine Pass, 26 February 1943.

The first clash of British and German forces in Tunisia came at Medjez el Bab on 17 November and ended Allied hopes of winning the race for Tunis. The British 11th and 36th Brigades were unable to break through the cordon established by a new German Fifth Panzer Army commanded by General von Arnim. Heavy rainfall hampered both sides. In turn, the British were able to hold a series of German counterattacks in January. Lieutenant General Anderson, who now commanded the Allied Tunisian Front, established three corps – British V, Free French XIX, and US II – in strong positions in the mountainous terrain from which he could launch a push in March. As it happened, however, it was the Germans who were to attack first as Rommel and von Arnim were persuaded by the German Commander in Chief in the Mediterranean, Field Marshal Albert Kesselring, to bury personal differences in order to try for a breakthrough in southern Tunisia. On 14 February 1943 as von Arnim attacked through the Faid Pass with 10th and 21st Panzer Divisions, Rommel advanced through Gafsa toward Kasserine. Continuing differences between the two German commanders and shortage of fuel halted Rommel by 22 February but the offensive inflicted a sharp shock to the US II Corps which suffered 6500 casualties, and lost 183 tanks and 208 guns in the battle.

Rommel had won some time in the west but he was then repulsed when he attempted to envelop the Eighth Army at Medenine in the east on 6-7 March, ULTRA having provided Montgomery with both date and operational details. On 9 March Rommel went to Germany on sick leave and it was von Arnim who was left to defend the shrinking 'Tunis box.' Montgomery outflanked the Mareth Line on 20 March and forced the Germans back on Enfidaville. After heavy fighting this was taken on 20 April

Malta GC

With the loss of Greece and Crete and the arrival of the Afrika Korps in North Africa, the British colony of Malta became of crucial importance to the Allies as both a naval and air base from which to strike at Axis shipping. In fact, even the capture of Malta would not have materially assisted the German logistic problems in North Africa for the capacity of Libyan ports was so limited that it would have made no difference to the length of German lines of communication in the desert. However, Malta's potential threat to the security of the Afrika Korps brought it under heavy aerial attack from January 1941 onward although this eased with the diversion of German resources to the Aegean in May and to Russia in June. This respite enabled the island's fighter defenses to be strengthened – there had been only 15 on the island in January and, despite re-

inforcements being flown in, losses had been heavy. Then the German attack was resumed with a vengeance in March 1942, April being the peak month for destruction around Valletta and its harbor and docks. The Maltese, who took refuge in the island's caves during the raids, were subjected to enormous privation as the Royal Navy attempted to run the gauntlet of air attack to bring in convoys of supplies. In tribute to the islanders' fortitude, King George VI awarded the island the George Cross on 16 April 1942 but the ordeal continued. Sufficient supplies were received in the Pedestal convoy of August 1942 to keep the island going until December and the Stoneage and Portcullis convoys in November and December 1942 respectively then provided enough to maintain the island until the defeat of the German forces in Tunisia.

but the main Allied breakthrough came in the Medjerda valley on 6 May. Alexander, whose 18th Army Group included the British First and Eighth Armies and the US II Corps, now directed the British 6th Armored Division to make a moonlit attack from Hammam Lif to Hammamet to deny the Germans access to any last refuge on Cape Bon. With no chance to escape, von Arnim's forces capitulated. In all, 248,000 German and Italian troops were taken between 6 and 13 May.

BELOW: Some of the thousands of German and Italian troops held in Allied compounds after the final collapse of Axis resistance in Tunisia.

With the entire shore of North Africa free of Axis forces, the Allies were poised to launch an invasion of Sicily, this next step having been agreed at the Casablanca Conference in January in preference to an earlier cross-Channel invasion of northwest Europe. While the Americans tended to view Sicily as the limit of their Mediterranean objectives prior to re-entry to France – codenamed Operation Roundup – in 1944, the British declined to rule out subsequent ventures. Eisenhower had been appointed Supreme Commander for the invasion of Sicily – Operation Husky – at Casablanca while Alexander would direct the ground forces in a new 15th Army Group comprising Montgomery's Eighth Army and Patton's US Seventh Army. However, Montgomery refused to accept the original plan for two widely separated landings with the result that British and US forces were landed close together at the south and southeastern end of the island. The smaller island of Panatellaria was taken on 11 June after lengthy bombardment and aerial preparation for the main assault against Sicily began on 3 July.

Allied deception plans convinced Hitler that the Balkans rather than Sicily were the real objectives while, at lower level, the Italian Sixth Army was persuaded by similar means to dissipate its strength in the south by sending the German 15th Panzer Grenadier Division to the west. What was to be the largest amphibious assault of the war commenced with parachute and glider-borne descents by British and US forces on 10 July. Unexpected gusting winds and the inexperience of pilots caused the airborne forces to be widely scattered over land and sea. The seaborne assault was equally fraught with problems and confusion but there was virtually no opposition and the Italian defense collapsed. Once a more determined counter-attack – spearheaded by the German Hermann Goering Panzer Division – was beaten off by US forces at Gela on 11 June, the defenders retired on the Straits of Messina. By 17 August the Germans had extricated 39,000 men and the Italians some 70,000 troops.

On 26 July King Victor Emmanuel had demanded Mussolini's resignation and, placing the Italian dictator under arrest, the king appointed Marshal Badoglio as head of government. Two months before at the Washington Trident Conference, the Allies had considered extending operations in the Mediterranean since only seven divisions would need to be brought back to Britain for the cross-Channel invasion set for May 1944. Developments in Italy suggested that the Italians might collapse altogether if pushed and on 16 August Eisenhower decided on the most ambitious of eight possible schemes prepared by his staff for landings in Italy, and Operation Avalanche was approved by the Quadrant Conference at Quebec on the day the Germans completed the evacuation of Sicily. Negotiations were put in train with the Italians who agreed to surrender to the Allies on 3 September as Montgomery's Eighth Army made a diversionary assault (Operation Baytown) across the Straits of Messina. The announcement of the surrender was not made, however, until the morning of 8 September with Mark Clark's US Fifth Army at sea en route to the chosen objective of Avalanche, which was Salerno. Salerno was the northernmost beach that could be covered by Allied aircraft from Sicily. Early use of a major port was also a necessity and landing there offered the opportunity of outflanking Naples, which could not be taken by direct assault from the sea.

Unfortunately the Germans had anticipated the Italian desire to throw in the towel and their strength had been gradually increased to 16 divisions, Kesselring commanding Army Group C in southern Italy and Rommel commanding Army Group B in the north. Salerno itself had been occupied by the 16th Panzer Division which was well placed on high ground. Thus, there was no possibility of surprise and, although a beachhead was secured, the US

ABOVE: Men of the British 51st Highland Division come ashore on Sicily in July 1943.

ABOVE RIGHT: Churchill on his second visit to the Western Desert, 23 August 1942 with Alexander, Montgomery and Alanbrooke. Churchill advocated an all-out invasion of Italy once the war in the desert ended.

RIGHT: Consolidating the beachhead at Salerno on the Italian mainland. Note the American MP ducking to take cover from an incoming shell.

and British forces were unable to attain their first objectives. Between 10 and 13 September, while the Allies endeavored to land reinforcements, Kesselring disengaged from Montgomery in the south and concentrated five more divisions around Salerno. Massive Allied airpower finally blunted Kesselring's counterattacks, and on 16 September he withdrew toward the Volturno river. Montgomery linked with Clark that same day and, shifting its axis to the east coast, Eighth Army advanced on Bari on 22 September and on Foggia on 27 September.

Kesselring retired slowly to win time for further defense lines to be constructed behind him, notably the Gustav Line. The Germans were back on the Volturno by 7 October and had also abandoned Sardinia. Hitler was

undecided as to whether to defend on the Volturno or retire farther north, but in the end decided to order Kesselring to stand on the Volturno. This new resolve, conveyed to the Allies courtesy of ULTRA, necessitated further efforts to push the Germans north toward Rome. Under the pressure of continuing Allied advances, Kesselring quit the Volturno line on 15 October for the first of two temporary positions – the Barbara and Reinhard – at which he hoped to impose further delay. The onset of winter rains in October, the nature of the terrain and the determined fighting qualities of the German divisions ensured that the Allies did not reach the forward defenses of the Gustav Line until January 1944. The Allied attacks on the line would see heavy fighting.

FAR LEFT: Patton, the commander of the US Third Army, in conversation with Lieutenant Colonel Bernard of the 30th Infantry Regiment, 3rd Infantry Division, in Sicily.

BELOW, FAR LEFT: Allied wounded from the Sicilian campaign are evacuated from Syracuse.

BELOW: Landing craft from USS Andromeda head for the beach at Salerno on 9 September 1943.

By now the pressing logistic demands of cross-Channel invasion – since renamed Operation Overlord – meant that 68 vital landing craft known as Landing Ship Tanks (LSTs) had to be speedily withdrawn from the Mediterranean. This jeopardized a plan drawn up by Eisenhower's staff (Operation Shingle) to crack the Gustav Line by launching an amphibious assault at Anzio south of Rome. The prospect of the Italian campaign coming to a halt enabled Churchill to persuade the Americans to agree to postpone despatch of the LSTs from 15 January to 5 February 1944, an earlier postponement from 15 December 1943 having been won at the Cairo-Tehran Sextant Conferences in November. Accordingly, Major General Lucas' US VI Corps was to land at Anzio on 22 January 1944, five days after the opening of Fifth Army's attack on the Gustav Line across the Garigliano and Rapido rivers. British X Corps made only limited progress when it opened the attack on 17 January while US II Corps made none at all. Unfortunately the Anzio landing had not only been hastily prepared but Lucas also had a more limited view of what he was supposed to achieve than either Clark at Fifth Army or Alexander at 15th Army Group. Thus, although Lucas met no opposition at Anzio, he chose to dig in to consolidate the beachhead rather than advance inland. By the time Lucas did advance on 30 January Kesselring had been able to scrape together sufficient reserves to block it and impose a virtual siege. Hitler ordered counterattacks against Anzio in February and March but these were blunted by Allied airpower and ended on 3 March. An opportunity had certainly been missed and the need to keep supplying Anzio forced yet another postponement to Overlord and the near cancellation of a supporting operation – Anvil – in the south of France.

The key to further success in Italy was now Monte Cassino, the monastery dominating the Rapido valley. A first Allied attempt to seize it on 24 January had failed; then another between 29 January and 4 February. On 15 February the Allies leveled the monastery with bombs only to discover that the rubble had become an even more formidable obstacle. The New Zealand 2nd Division made

Monte Cassino

Crowned by a famous monastery, Monte Cassino rose 1700 feet above the Rapido valley and dominated Route 8 – the ancient Via Casilina – to Rome. Consequently it had become one of the cardinal points of the Gustav Line. The Germans did not occupy the monastery itself but had well-prepared defensive positions which they hoped would offset Allied superiority in manpower and materiel. Indeed, the German lack of manpower made it necessary to leave units in the front line without relief for long periods, and the German 1st Parachute Division fought at Cassino continuously for 220 days. Through the determination of the defenders, it would take the Allies six months and four separate 'battles' to break Cassino. In the first (17 January to 12 February) the US 34th Division failed to take Monastery Hill and was then relieved by the 4th Indian and New Zealand Divisions. On 15 February 1944 142 B-17s dropped 350 tons of bombs on the monastery as well as incendiaries as a prelude to the second battle (15 to 17 February) but the Indians and New Zealanders also failed to carry the hill. Once more aircraft were used, over 500 bombers dropping 1250 tons on Cassino and 748 artillery pieces joining in with over 195,000 round on 15 March prior to the third assault (15 to 23 March) in which the Indians and New Zealanders were again repulsed. Finally, an attempt was made to outflank the defenses rather than try another frontal assault and in the fourth battle (11 to 20 May) the 12th Podolski Regiment of the Polish II Corps carried the objective on 18 May 1944.

Monte Cassino pictured after a heavy Allied artillery bombardment.

the third abortive attack on 17 February. A further aerial and artillery bombardment was delivered on 15 March but again the New Zealanders failed. Alexander now paused and undertook a major reorganization to transfer all US units to Fifth Army in the west and all British and Imperial formations to Eighth Army in the east. While a deception plan had led Kesselring to expect another amphibious assault, Eighth Army then launched a major attack in the Liri valley (Operation Diadem) on 11 May, and VI Corps at Anzio made diversionary attacks. This time the advance succeeded, with the Free French Corps breaking through the Gustav Line and the Polish Corps carrying the ruins of Cassino on 17 May. Clark failed to cut off Kesselring's retreat by his decision to seize Rome, which fell to the Allies on 4 June, and the Germans were able to retreat toward further defensive positions on the Gothic Line.

ABOVE: German heavy field artillery in action in Italy.

RIGHT: The Allied entry into Rome, the first Axis capital to fall to the Allies. Highlanders lead the victory parade.

ABOVE LEFT: New Zealanders, armed with machine guns and range-finders, shoot up the slopes of Monte Cassino, March 1944.

LEFT: British troops pass through their own positions during the advance on San Angelo in May 1944.

Somewhat unexpectedly, US Fifth Army broke through the Gothic Line in mid-September 1944, Kesselring having lost four of his best divisions to the south of France and having transferred seven others to face Eighth Army in the east. However, the Allies had also lost divisions to the operation in the south of France – now renamed Operation Dragoon – and efforts were also sabotaged by the rains. There were only minor operations during the winter months, the Germans achieving one local success when overrunning the relatively inexperienced American 92nd Division in December.

By the spring of 1945 the Allied armies were ready to re-open the offensive and, with close support from bombers, Eighth Army attacked on 9 April and Fifth Army five days later. The Allies were across the Po by 20 April and eight days later Kesselring's successor, General von Vieting-hoff, surrendered. The German capitulation came into effect on 2 May 1945. On the day Vietinghoff agreed to surrender Mussolini met his death. He had been rescued by the Germans from detention at Gran Sasso on 12 September 1943 but now fell into the hands of Italian partisans near Lake Como and he and his mistress were executed.

Alexander was to claim that the Italian campaign had tied down 55 German divisions at the time of the Normandy invasion although, in fact, there were only 26 divisions in Italy. Moreover, while the Germans had not been able to deploy these divisions elsewhere, their tenacious defense had ensured that the Allies were committed to continuing a campaign which could only be of secondary importance in Hitler's defeat. Nor would it have been logistically or geographically possible for the Allies to have launched a rapid advance to reach Vienna from Italy in 1944 in order to forestall the Soviets as has sometimes been suggested.

To some extent, the Italian campaign had frustrated Allied plans elsewhere in the Mediterranean as well as delaying D-Day. Planning for a landing in the south of France had been entrusted to US Seventh Army under Lieutenant General Patch. Churchill had never liked the idea and was attempting to cancel it as late as August 1944, first believing that the troops might be used more profitably in the Balkans and later in western France. The Germans expected an invasion in the south and retained ten divisions there but a deception plan convinced them

TOP: *Prisoners from the German 117th Infantry Regiment, taken during the battle for the Gothic Line.*

ABOVE: *An American armored column pauses at the outskirts of Milan.*

FAR LEFT: *Soldiers of the US 598th Field Artillery Battery fire their 105mm howitzers against targets across the Arno, 29 August 1944.*

LEFT: *Mussolini after his rescue from Gran Sasso by Otto Skorzeny (left), 12 September 1943.*

TOP RIGHT: *Abandoned victims of a German pill-box on the Aquino-Pontecorvo road, June 1944.*

ABOVE RIGHT: *Led by communist forces of ELAS, a British column enters Corinth in Greece.*

RIGHT: *Yugoslav partisans burying German dead.*

that Genoa was the real target. Operation Dragoon then went ahead on 15 August 1944 with both Toulon and Marseilles secured by the Free French II Corps by 28 August and the Germans forced to fall back. French forces linked with the US Third Army advancing from Normandy near Dijon on 12 September and the French I and II Corps were then merged into a First French Army under General de Lattre de Tassigny to continue the final stages of the liberation of their country.

While Churchill had disliked Dragoon, a favorite project was the capture of the Italian Dodecanese islands including Rhodes as a base from which to help the Greek and Yugoslav partisans, attack Rumania and influence Turkey. The Americans in turn disliked this, but after the Italian surrender British forces occupied the smaller islands in September 1943. A descent on Rhodes was also planned but Hitler was not prepared to yield so easily, and German forces including airborne troops bundled the British off Kos on 3 October and from Leros between 12 and 16 November. Churchill tried but failed to get Rhodes put back on the Allied agenda at the Cairo and Tehran Conferences but failed to sway the Americans who showed equal disinterest in Greece.

In Greece, the main beneficiary of the Italian collapse had been the Greek National Liberation Army (ELAS), the military wing of the communist National Liberation Front (EAM). ELAS now became better armed than its nationalist rival, the National Democratic Greek League (EDES), between whom and ELAS civil war erupted in October 1943. Churchill was determined that Greece should not fall into communist hands when the Germans withdrew and on 4 October 1944 British troops were landed at Patrai in support of the royalist government in exile. The Germans evacuated Athens and British troops entered it on 14 October. Churchill had exacted a pledge from Stalin not to interfere and went to Athens himself on Christmas Day to oversee negotiations between the Greek government and ELAS, which had clashed with British troops in early December. Having been driven out of Athens by the British, ELAS signed the Varkiza Agreement on 12 February 1945 accepting demobilization in return for an amnesty, a plebiscite on the country's future and a general election.

Farther north in Yugoslavia, communist guerrillas had also benefited from the Italian capitulation since they were able to disarm the ten Italian divisions in the country. Resistance to the Germans had begun almost at once with largely spontaneous uprisings in Montenegro and Slovenia in July 1941. It spread as the bulk of the German forces were withdrawn for the Russian campaign and on 22 December 1941 the communists had formed their 1st Proletarian Brigade as a nucleus of a regular army of partisans. By 1943 the communists had between 200,000 and 300,000 men and a political network throughout the country presided over by Josip Broz (Tito). The situation was complicated, however, by the country's national rivalries, the pro-Nazi Croatian *Ustashas* fighting alongside the Germans and the largely royalist Serbian *Cetniks* of Draza Mihailovich edging ever closer to collaboration with the Italians and Germans against the communists. Initially, Mihailovich won Allied recognition but Tito assumed this mantle in 1943 and received increasing material assistance. The Germans did not afford much importance to Yugoslavia and, although they directed seven major offensives at Tito's partisans between November 1941 and the summer of 1944, many of the troops employed were elderly or second-rate. For all that it was a brutal struggle until Soviet troops crossed the frontier from Bulgaria and Rumania in a co-ordinated drive with Tito's forces. Tito entered Belgrade on 27 October 1944, mounted a further offensive along the Adriatic coast, and on 30 April 1945 entered the long-contested port of Trieste. The Balkans too were clear of German troops.

CHAPTER FIVE

STRUGGLE FOR AIR SUPREMACY

It has been suggested that the armed forces of Europe between the two world wars were not unlike ancient mariners navigating by dead reckoning, unable to verify their calculations and always extrapolating upon past experience. The further from the last relevant experience, the greater the chances of error. They were also bureaucracies and shared a common tendency to be unreceptive to new ideas, which equally led to planning upon preconceived lessons from the past. In such circumstances, it did not necessarily matter if the planners had got it wrong, only that they adapted themselves sufficiently quickly to get it right. There can be no better example of these themes than the theories of airpower current in the interwar years, which were all assumptions based on the briefest operational experience during World War I.

The first real use of airpower for strategic bombing was the raids by the British Royal Naval Air Service on the German Zeppelin sheds at Cologne and Düsseldorf in late 1914 followed by the first large-scale Zeppelin raid upon the British east-coast resort of Great Yarmouth on 19 January 1915. Zeppelins dropped a total of 200 tons of bombs over England in 51 raids before losses – mostly due to crash landings – brought a switch to new Gotha heavy aircraft. Gothas made a further 57 raids, the most notable being that on 13 June 1917 when 14 aircraft dropped 118 bombs on London in the vicinity of Liverpool Street Station. They caused 600 casualties including 160 dead, all the bombers returning home safely despite the efforts of over 100 British fighters to intercept them. The raid caused near panic in official circles engendering fears of a defenseless capital and a collapse of domestic morale. Squadrons were pulled back from France but the Germans were able to conduct another successful raid three weeks later.

The British Cabinet established a sub-committee of the Committee of Imperial Defense which recommended the establishment of an independent bombing force, the Royal Air Force (RAF), since it concluded that the only means of defense lay in attack. The committee, chaired by the South African statesman Jan Smuts, also concluded

that bombing of civilians would have devastating effects in the future. Indeed, if 14 aircraft had achieved so much, what might a larger force do? In turn, the Royal Flying Corps (RFC) and the RAF, which was formally set up on 1 April 1918, dropped some 665 tons of bombs on Germany between October 1917 and November 1918 but 137 aircraft were lost or became missing and 325 destroyed or wrecked. On the night of 11 November 1918 three new Handley Page bombers were waiting to bomb Berlin but the armistice intervened. In reality, World War I neither proved nor disproved the theories of the Smuts Committee but all subsequent concepts became a crude multiplication of the effects of the Gotha raids. The RAF and its first Chief of Staff, Lord Trenchard, assumed the bomber would always get through because of the sheer difficulties of locating hostile aircraft. The fighters developed in the interwar years remained primitive until the emergence of eight- or 12-gun monoplanes in the late 1930s. There was also no operational experience on which to draw, apart from the RAF's 'aerial policing' against tribesmen in the Middle East, Africa, and on the Indian Northwest Frontier. Later the raids upon Guernica and other Spanish towns by the Luftwaffe's Condor Legion during the Spanish Civil War also seemed to emphasize the effect of bombing upon morale. Trenchard had also been concerned to press the dangers inherent in aerial attack in the interests of the RAF's institutional survival amid financial retrenchment in interwar Britain. Similar assumptions were being made in other countries by other outspoken advocates of strategic bombing such as Billy Mitchell in the United States, Walter Wever in Germany, and Guilo Douhet in Italy.

Thus, in 1939 there were frightening calculations being made as to the extent of likely casualties from bombing. It was thought that someone could be killed by a blast pressure of 5lbs per square inch. In fact, the war showed there was a 50 percent chance of survival even with a blast pressure of 500lbs per square inch. It was also believed in Britain that the Luftwaffe could drop at least 700 tons a day with a massive opening assault of 3500 tons in the first

PREVIOUS PAGES: Pilots of the RAF's No 1 Squadron scramble to their Hurricanes on a French airfield during the Battle for France.

ABOVE: Air Chief Marshal Sir Hugh Dowding, leader of Fighter Command in the Battle of Britain.

FAR RIGHT: The control room at RAF Fighter Command in the summer of 1940.

BELOW RIGHT: Senior RAF officers watch WRAF girls plotting aircraft in an operations room of Fighter Command.

BELOW: One of the vital radar 'chain home' stations on the east coast of England.

24 hours. An earlier calculation of a rate of 600 tons a day had suggested 150,000 casualties in the first week and by 1939 it was assumed that there would be upward of four million psychological casualties alone in the first six months of a war. As early as 1931 plans had been made to evacuate women and children from London and other urban and coastal cities. Curiously, it was assumed that the RAF could not retaliate sufficiently and that its raids would only provoke further retaliation, a clear case of a presumed deterrent being most effectively deterred. In any case, the government was unwilling to attack other than military targets (the Chancellor of the Exchequer in Chamberlain's Cabinet, Sir Kingsley Wood, reputedly opposed using incendiaries against the Black Forest on the grounds that it was private property). Bomber Command was restricted to propaganda flights which, according to Sir Arthur Harris, merely supplied the continent's toilet paper requirements for the next five years. Moreover, there was no opening German onslaught.

The reason was that the Luftwaffe had not developed as a strategic bombing force. Wever had died in an air crash in 1936 and thereafter the Luftwaffe became an auxiliary to the army, geared to providing it with tactical battlefield support with its medium bombers (the Heinkel 111 and Dornier 217), a strategic fighter (the Messerschmidt 110) and the Stuka dive bomber. For the Luftwaffe the lesson of Spain was that bombing cities made little impact; it was far more important to catch one's opponent's airforce on the ground. Conversely, the attention given to the medium bomber and dive bomber led to a neglect of fighter aircraft, the Messerschmidt 109 being virtually forced on the Luftwaffe through the sheer determination of its designer. This meant that when it was required to undertake a battle for the command of the skies over Britain in 1940 the Luftwaffe was hopelessly ill-equipped for such a strategic role. In any case, it was given the quite separate tasks of blockading Britain, winning air superiority, and defeating Britain by a simultaneous independent air offensive.

The RAF was equally badly placed through the loss of 25 percent of its fighter aircraft – 432 planes – in France in May and June. Churchill finally had had to decide on 19 May not to send any more fighters abroad after Air Chief Marshal Sir Hugh Dowding of Fighter Command had said he could no longer guarantee air security. Fortunately some priority had been accorded since 1935 to the development of Sir Robert Watson-Watt's work on radar and a chain of installations had been constructed along the coast of England by 1940. With a range not far short of that of the Luftwaffe fighters, the radar stations could provide an accurate picture of German intentions. Dowding, who had come to Fighter Command from RAF Research and Development in 1936, had also organized a highly effec-

Strategic Bombing

The most celebrated advocate of strategic bombing was the Italian Guilo Douhet (1869-1930), an artillery officer whose interest in airpower was such that he was court-martialed in 1916 for the strength of his advocacy of an independent air force in the Italian orbat. However, he was recalled to head the Central Aeronautical Bureau in 1918. Italy had pioneered bombing from aircraft in Libya prior to World War I when fighting against Turks and Libyan irregulars, and another Italian named Salvaneschi produced a work, *Let Us Kill the War: Let Us Aim at the Heart of the Enemy*, in 1917 that argued a decisive blow could be struck from the air.

Douhet's own book, *The Command of the Air*, was published in Italy in 1921 and translated into French in 1932, into German in 1935 and into English in the following year. Douhet saw no distinction in modern war between a belligerent and a non-belligerent; he also believed that the experience of World War I proved that land warfare could no longer be decisive and was destined to result in continual stalemate. Consequently, aircraft offered a means of by-passing that stalemate by flying over armies and navies and striking directly at the heartland of an enemy state. Armies and navies would be rendered largely superfluous by air forces. The speed and elevation of the aircraft themselves ensured that there would be no adequate defense and the bomber, which was the only aircraft Douhet was concerned with, would always get through to the target. A sustained aerial attack on the enemy centers of population, government, and industry using high explosives,

incendiaries and poison gas would shatter morale and force the enemy to sue for peace. Moreover, an air force would be able to achieve the command of the air necessary to achieve this result by a preliminary offensive at an enemy's aerial resources.

Douhet was clearly writing before the invention of radar when it still appeared that effective air defense was impossible. It could also be argued that the use of air-delivered poison gas might also have made a greater impact upon civilian morale in World War II than using high explosives and incendiaries. Nevertheless, Douhet still grossly overestimated the physical effects per ton of bombs dropped and suggested that no more than 500 tons would be sufficient to destroy a large city and reduce its inhabitants to terrified subjection.

There were other theorists of airpower although the American aviator, Billy Mitchell, and the former Russian pilot, Alexander de Seversky (whose *Victory Through Air Power* was published in the United States in 1942 and was turned into an animated film by Walt Disney the following year), were less original in their thought and were more concerned to promote airpower in general rather than strategic bombing in particular. In Britain Lord Trenchard was influential in the development of the RAF's strategic bombing theory. With so many theorists working in parallel the true impact of Douhet's views is hard to assess, but all this interest added to the prevailing assumptions about the effectiveness of the air weapon.

tive command and control system for handling radar, observer, and ULTRA intelligence, and for mobilizing fighter resources to meet the threats as they developed. A third advantage was the development of Sidney Camm's Hurricane and R J Mitchell's Spitfire, aircraft ironically given priority by civil servants rather than the RAF when British rearmament had begun in earnest in the 1930s. The British fighters were not necessarily superior to the Bf 109 in all respects, but they would be operating well within their range when the latter had but ten minutes flying time over London and southeast England.

The battle which became known as the Battle of Britain began on 10 July 1940 with Luftwaffe attacks on Channel shipping. These did little damage and not only failed to draw out the RAF but also gave Dowding longer in which to train pilots and take delivery of new aircraft. Delayed by bad weather, the Luftwaffe launched *Adlertag* ('Eagle Day') on 13 August, switching the offensive to RAF airfields with secondary night attacks on cities. The radar station at Ventnor was put out of action for 11 days but the Luftwaffe failed to recognize the significance of the radar towers, and there were also major internal disagreements on the correct tactics the Luftwaffe should adopt. The British also had their disagreements. Air Vice-Marshal Keith Park of No 11 Group favored small formations and Leigh-Mallory of No 12 Group called for 'big wings' of aircraft to hit the German bomber formations. Park was certainly correct in responding more flexibly. Both he and Dowding were unjustly dismissed in November 1940, and when Leigh-Mallory's tactics were implemented they were largely ineffective, although the battle had been long won by this time.

In fact, the Luftwaffe came close to success as RAF losses mounted through August. Then, on 24 August, a Luftwaffe bomber's load was released over London by mistake. Churchill demanded retaliation on Berlin, a somewhat abortive mission being carried out on the next night. But the few bombs that fell on his capital infuriated Hitler and on 4 September he demanded the bombing of London in revenge. The Luftwaffe began the new mission on 7 September but it lacked the means to carry out a strategic bombing role, mainly because it had no night bomb-aiming device and little night flying experience. The Germans had also erred in using their relatively sophisticated *Knickebein* navigational device – guiding aircraft to targets by radio beams – at an early stage of the battle; the British had learned how to jam it before the Luftwaffe switched to night attack. Above all the switch

RIGHT: Much like their RAF counterparts, Luftwaffe pilots await orders during the Battle of Britain. .

LEFT: A downed German pilot is interrogated by a village policeman and local defense force members.

CENTER LEFT: Rearming a Spitfire Mk 1A of No 19 Squadron at Duxford in September 1940.

BELOW, FAR LEFT: A familiar image of the Battle of Britain.

BELOW LEFT: One of the top Luftwaffe aces, Adolf Galland.

BELOW: A Luftwaffe Heinkel 111 medium bomber brought down over Scotland early in the war.

to London gave the RAF the respite it needed, and when the Germans made one last major daylight effort on 15 September they failed. It was claimed at the time that the Germans had lost 185 aircraft – the real figure was 57 compared to 27 RAF airplanes but this was just as decisive. The worst day's losses had been the 71 German aircraft lost compared to 29 RAF aircraft on 15 August, but the September raids marked the end of the Luftwaffe's attempt to win air superiority. It had lost a total of over 1100 aircraft of all types and the RAF some 650 aircraft.

The outcome of the battle actually proved the theorists of airpower wrong since a supposedly strategic airforce had not overcome a fighter defense. The bombing of London and other cities by the Luftwaffe – the Italians also contributed aircraft with raids mostly on east-coast towns – failed to crack British morale even though the raids continued until 16 May 1941. There was occasional panic, as in West Ham when the local authorities demanded a complete evacuation after a raid on 11 September 1940: in the event, only 3000 accepted the offer. There were also similar difficulties in Coventry when local organization broke down in the wake of a raid on 14 November 1940 in which 554 people were killed and 865 seriously injured. However, provincial raids were too erratic to do permanent damage and in London it would appear that people simply got used to the bombing. Only four percent of Londoners used the London Underground stations as shelters, nine percent used other public shelters, 27 percent used shelters in their own homes, and the remainder either did not bother to take shelter or stayed in their own homes with

ABOVE: Londoners share a communal shelter during the height of the Blitz.

ABOVE RIGHT: St Paul's Cathedral rises majestically above the surrounding destruction during a heavy attack on London.

ABOVE, FAR RIGHT: London's docks ablaze after the first large-scale daylight raid on 7 September 1940.

LEFT: A Heinkel He 111 over London during the Battle of Britain.

RIGHT: Coventry the morning after the bombing of November 1940. Much of the city center was destroyed in this raid – one of the heaviest attacks on a provincial center.

no special precautions. Total casualties to bombing in Britain throughout the war at 51,509 dead were far less than any of the prewar predictions.

Yet the lessons of the Battle of Britain and the London 'Blitz' did not sway the advocates of strategic bombing, which remained the RAF's *raison d'être*; but there had been curiously little study of how a bombing offensive might be carried out in practice. The so-called 'Western Air Plans' of 1939-40 envisaged precision bombing of military targets, especially plants for synthetic oil production, by day. But Bomber Command lacked the aircraft, equipment and experience to carry out such attacks in face of the German air defenses. On 18 December 1939, for example, 12 out of 22 Wellingtons had been lost in a daylight attack on Wilhelmshaven when set upon by ME 109s and 110s. As a result on 19 March 1940 the RAF switched to night precision attacks with a raid on Hornum, but these proved even less successful in the absence of adequate navigational aids. Only a third of the bombs dropped fell within five miles of targets and only ten percent within two miles; enthusiasm for attacking oil production had also waned by the time the RAF was released from attacks on German naval targets in July 1941. These factors caused Air Marshal Harris, who had taken over Bomber Command in February 1942, to switch to area bombing by night on 14 February 1942. It was the only policy open to the RAF which was likely to achieve anything at all when no other direct British retaliation against Germany was possible. Thus, on 30-31 May 1942 Bomber Command launched Operation Millennium ('the 1000-Bomber Raid') on Cologne. There had been earlier raids on Essen, Lübeck and Rostock in which the new GEE radar system had been used to guide pathfinders to target areas where they dropped flares and incendiaries to mark the target for the following waves of the main force and this now allowed 1048 aircraft to be assembled over the city. The results were negligible with 469 Germans killed and 39 aircraft lost but it did much for British morale and showed the Allies, neutrals and European resistance movements alike that Britain could hit back. By contrast, the limited raids mounted by the RAF on Italy from 3 June 1940 onward were rather more successful in hitting industrial targets at Milan, Genoa and Turin.

Partly the result of frustration, area bombing was nonetheless intended to dislocate German industry, power plant and communications by destroying the cities associated with them. The United States Eighth Air Force also entered the fray in 1942 but the Americans were unim-

LEFT: The Handley Page Halifax bomber was one of the mainstays of RAF Bomber Command.

BELOW LEFT: RAF Wellingtons over the Western Desert during the early war years.

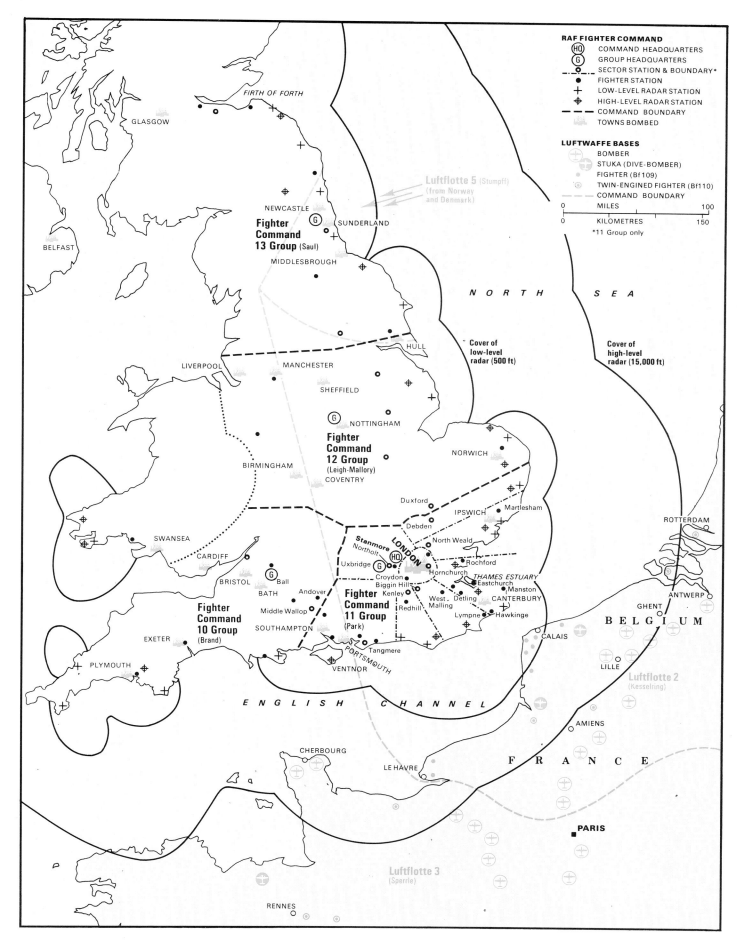

RAF FIGHTER COMMAND
- (HO) COMMAND HEADQUARTERS
- (G) GROUP HEADQUARTERS
- SECTOR STATION & BOUNDARY*
- • FIGHTER STATION
- + LOW-LEVEL RADAR STATION
- ⊕ HIGH-LEVEL RADAR STATION
- COMMAND BOUNDARY
- TOWNS BOMBED

LUFTWAFFE BASES
- BOMBER
- STUKA (DIVE-BOMBER)
- FIGHTER (Bf 109)
- TWIN-ENGINED FIGHTER (Bf 110)
- COMMAND BOUNDARY

MILES 0 — 100
KILOMETRES 0 — 150
*11 Group only

FIRTH OF FORTH

GLASGOW

BELFAST

NEWCASTLE

Luftflotte 5 (Stumpff)
(from Norway and Denmark)

Fighter Command 13 Group (Saul)

SUNDERLAND

MIDDLESBROUGH

NORTH SEA

HULL

Cover of low-level radar (500 ft)

Cover of high-level radar (15,000 ft)

LIVERPOOL

MANCHESTER

SHEFFIELD

NOTTINGHAM

Fighter Command 12 Group (Leigh-Mallory)

NORWICH

BIRMINGHAM

COVENTRY

Duxford

Debden

IPSWICH

Martlesham

ROTTERDAM

SWANSEA

North Weald

Stanmore
Northolt
LONDON

CARDIFF

Uxbridge (G) (HO)

Croydon
Biggin Hill
Kenley
Redhill

Hornchurch

Rochford

THAMES ESTUARY
Eastchurch
Manston

ANTWERP

BRISTOL

Ball (G)

West Malling

Detling

CANTERBURY

GHENT

BATH

Andover

Lympne

Hawkinge

BELGIUM

Middle Wallop

Fighter Command 11 Group (Park)

Fighter Command 10 Group (Brand)

SOUTHAMPTON

Tangmere

CALAIS

LILLE

Luftflotte 2 (Kesselring)

EXETER

PORTSMOUTH

VENTNOR

PLYMOUTH

ENGLISH CHANNEL

AMIENS

CHERBOURG

FRANCE

LE HAVRE

FAR LEFT: 'Window' aluminium foil being manufactured; a device used to deceive Germany's radar defenses during the Allied bomber offensive.

LEFT: B-24 Liberators of the 15th USAAF over the Ploesti oil refineries in Rumania, 31 May 1944.

Luftflotte 3 (Sperrle)

PARIS

RENNES

pressed with British efforts and in the classic Douhet mold believed that they could fight their way to a target in daylight using heavily armed high-altitude B-17 bombers. Their first raid was on the marshaling yards at Rouen on 17 August 1942. But effective bombing was in direct proportion to the effectiveness of the air defenses and a maximum effort could not be achieved until the German air defenses were beaten. Area bombing by night could not do this because it would not bring about a decisive battle as the strategy's success depended on bombers avoiding the enemy defenses or reducing their effectiveness through dispersed attacks. Moreover, the GEE system was as vulnerable to German jamming as *Knickebein* and its later variants had been to British interference. A more

advanced H$_2$S radar and the 'Oboe' system were both introduced by the RAF, which also developed a variety of methods to jam German defensive radar such as 'Jostle,' and 'Window,' the latter being strips of foil cut to match radar wavelengths to produce a mass of false targets when released. But even these did not enable the RAF to take on the German defenses. Similarly, the Americans could not do so by day because, however well armed, the B-17 was a bomber and not a fighter. Despite its defensive formations, the USAAF suffered crippling losses amounting to nearly ten percent by October 1943.

Both RAF and USAAF attempted major efforts to bring about a decisive blow during 1943. The Americans suffered major disasters. Sixty-one out of 178 aircraft were

ABOVE: British and German dispositions during the Battle of Britain in the summer of 1940.

The Dams Raid

The idea to attack the dams which supplied water to German heavy industry originated in a paper by the brilliant scientist Barnes Wallis in March 1941. An Air Attack on Dams Committee was formed but it concluded that the prime objective – the Möhne dam – was too strong to be destroyed by conventional bombing. Wallis, however, conceived of a bouncing bomb which would rebound off the dam wall and sink to a required depth of 30 feet in order to achieve maximum assistance from water pressure when it exploded. The bomb could be set off by hydrostatic fuse but the difficulty was to ensure that it sank close to the wall. Wallis solved this by having the bomb spin backwards as it left the aircraft and thus sinking forward when it hit the wall. The special bomb, 'Upkeep,' which was 50 inches × 60 inches and packed with 6600lbs of explosive, was to be held in a V-shaped bomb release mechanism which had a small motor to rotate the bomb prior to delivery. The bomb also had to be dropped at exactly 220mph and at a height of 60 feet above the water 425 yards from the wall of the dam. This problem was overcome by fixing spotlights at the nose and tail of the aircraft at such an angle that the beams met when the plane was 60 feet above the water and by using a triangular wooden sight with nails to enable the bomb aimer to line up the two towers on the dam at the correct range for release. No 617 Squadron RAF was formed specifically for the raid under command of Wing Commander Guy Gibson. Extensive training was undertaken for Operation Chastise on 16 May 1943 in which 19 Lancasters with 135 crew attacked the Möhne, Eder and Sorpe dams. A total of nine aircraft and 56 crew were lost but both the Möhne and the Eder dams were breached and the Sorpe damaged. Gibson received the Victoria Cross and there was widespread flooding but the raid did not result in long-term loss of industrial production for all its technical brilliance.

lost on a raid against the Ploesti oil fields in Rumania while 60 were lost over the Schweinfurt ball-bearing plant on 17 August. In October, another 148 aircraft were lost in a week over Schweinfurt. The RAF's 'Battle for Berlin' saw 16 major attacks on the German capital between October 1943 and March 1944 amounting to 20,224 sorties but it cost 1047 aircraft. The Allies badly needed the respite from strategic bombing forced on them by the need to divert bombers to assist preparations for the invasion of Normandy. Eisenhower as Supreme Commander took strategic direction of the bombers from 1 April 1944 and it was hardly a moment too soon. Indeed, Bomber Command's last effort to prove its capabilities before being allocated to Eisenhower – the raid on Nuremburg on 30-31 March – was a major failure in which 97 out of 782 aircraft were lost to little effect.

The use of airpower against German forces in France was immensely successful in disrupting the transportation system with at least 18,000 workers being diverted from work on German defenses to repair railways and other communications in May 1944. As Supreme Commander, Eisenhower also employed aircraft for carpet bombing of ground targets in the subsequent campaign, a use the advocates of strategic bombing found irksome in the extreme, and it was not until late in the summer that Eisenhower relinquished control of the bombers. His deputy, Air Chief Marshal Sir Arthur Tedder, now suggested extending this style of attack to Germany's communications system, but Harris continued to press for area bombing while General Spaatz, who had taken over Eighth Air Force in January 1944, wanted to concentrate on Germany's synthetic oil industry. There was no Combined Strategic Targets Committee until September 1944 and even then the disagreements on priorities continued, efforts being dispersed between oil, transport, cities, and V-weapon sites.

At least one advantageous development had now occurred with the arrival of the North American P-51 Mustang, which was not only capable of accompanying the bombers over Germany when equipped with drop-tanks but also of outclassing any of the German air defense fighters. German forward radar sites, though never as efficient as British installations – the Heidelberg set with a range of 240 miles only entered service in 1944 – were also

RIGHT: A reconnaissance photograph of the Leipzig marshaling yards after an Allied air attack in early 1945.

LEFT: Identifying the dead after an Allied raid on a German city.

LEFT: The center of Berlin between the Tiergarten and the Zoological Gardens snapped by an RAF reconnaissance flight on 8 March 1945.

BELOW: Child victims of a bombing raid on Germany. Strategic bombing remains a controversial subject to the present.

The V-Weapons

As early as 1938 the Wehrmacht established a rocket-testing center at Pennemünde under the direction of Dr Walter Dornberger, the original suggestion having been made by the scientist Werner von Braun. Work had actually begun much earlier and a prototype A-1 rocket was tested in 1933. However, rivalries delayed the army project and it did not receive any priority until 1940. By October 1942 the latest A-4 prototype had been successfully fired over 100 miles and over 240 miles by 1943. The British had received indications of the work going on in 1939 but the significance was discounted until further reports were obtained through foreign laborers employed at Pennemünde and from aerial reconnaissance. As a result, the RAF first attacked the site in August 1943, setting back the project and persuading Hitler to give greater priority to the Luftwaffe's experimental flying bomb, a catapult-launched weapon codenamed Fi-103 but renamed by Hitler the *Vergeltungswaffe* ('Weapon of Retaliation'). Sites for the V-1 and V-3, a missile-firing gun, were constructed in France but so badly hit by Allied air attack that the V-3 was not used to attack Britain and the first V-1 attack was delayed until 16 June 1944. The delayed rocket project, now the V-2, made its first attack on London on 8 September 1944. In all, the V-1s and V-2s accounted for 6184 and 2754 deaths in Britain respectively (ten percent and 4.5 percent of all those killed by air or long-range bombardment) but they came too late to affect the outcome of the war. In the case of the V-1s, the sites themselves were soon overrun by the Allied advance from Normandy.

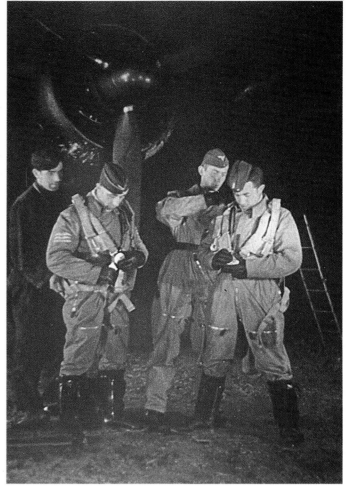

LEFT: Luftwaffe Stukas going into the attack during the Battle of Britain. Easy prey to RAF fighters, they were withdrawn from the battle.

TOP: A flight crew prepares for their next mission over Europe.

ABOVE: Luftwaffe fighter crews are briefed for a support mission over southern England.

RIGHT: Lancaster crews at an RAF station pose for the camera to celebrate a long-serving aircraft.

ABOVE RIGHT: Arming a German medium bomber – a small bomb-load made the He 111 a poor weapon for a strategic air offensive.

overrun in France. Thus, air superiority was won over Germany for the first time during 1944. But at the very moment when a maximum effort could now be delivered, the divergence of aims in the strategic bombing campaign delayed fulfillment of any. In any case, German industry was proving remarkably resilient. In 1943 Allied bombing had reduced production by only nine percent and even though three-quarters of all the tonnage dropped on Germany came after June 1944 the Germans still continued to increase production. That of tanks, self-propelled guns and assault guns did not peak until December 1944. Similarly, although every known air-frame plant in Germany was attacked by Allied aircraft from 20-25 February 1944 ('Big Week'), production rose from 2077 combat aircraft in January 1944 to 2243 in March and by September was twice that of January.

From the fall of 1944 onward, however, the Allies finally managed to sort out the targetting priorities for a concentrated attack on the oil industry and transportation. Production of synthetic oil fell rapidly from 662,000 tons a month in March 1944 to 80,000 tons a month in 1945. By 25 July 1944 Germany's armaments minister, Albert Speer, was urging total abandonment of all passenger and courier air services to conserve fuel, and the Ardennes offensive launched by the Wehrmacht in December 1944 had as one of its aims the capture of Allied fuel stocks. Production of aviation fuel was reduced by over 100,000 tons in one month alone and by March 1945 had virtually ceased altogether. Indeed, the Germans had barely suffi-

ABOVE: The devastating results of one Allied raid photographed by a pilot of the 363rd Tactical Reconnaissance Group of the USAAF.

LEFT: An ME 110 with night-flying radar being serviced by ground crews in Denmark before being sent to Britain for combat evaluation.

ABOVE: Incendiaries and high explosives fall toward the city of Dresden on 14 February 1945.

RIGHT: An RAF Halifax over the German synthetic oil plant at Wanne-Eickel in the Ruhr during the bomber offensive of 1944.

cient fuel left for normal day-to-day functioning of their armed forces. The assault on communications also began to cause severe dislocation by paralyzing the rapidly diminishing supply of raw materials, and steel production reached only four million tons in the last quarter of 1944 instead of the projected 37 million tons. Overall, German industrial production declined by between 30 and 40 percent over the period 1944 to 1945.

It is clear that area bombing had not had this effect; the tactic never reduced any city's industrial capacity by more than 60 percent and the Germans normally achieved a return to 80 percent production within three months. Nor did the strategic bombing campaign crack German morale which was just as resilient as that of the British under aerial attack. Only a third of the German population lived in cities and only one percent became casualties. Perhaps a fifth were cut off from water, gas, or electricity at one time or another, and one in 15 evacuated, but the majority escaped hardship. Some raids obviously made a deeper impression than others, such as those on Hamburg in July and August 1943; that on 2 August generated a fire storm and killed 42,000 people and caused up to a million to flee at least temporarily. Similarly, the raids on the communications center at Dresden in February 1945 ('Operation Thunderclap') resulted in possibly up to 135,000 dead, but overall the impact was not great. Berlin saw its population decline from four million in March 1943 to 2.9 million by March 1944 but the city continued to function until the Red Army overran it in April 1945. Habit was one factor in the German resilience, others were the nature of the state and the propaganda of Goebbels.

Certainly, the strategic bombing campaign had been the only means of striking back at Germany in 1940 and 1941. Nor is there any doubt that strategic airpower made D-Day possible, reduced the impact of Hitler's V-weapons and forced the Luftwaffe to concentrate on home defense rather than the Russian Front. It also diverted German resources – possibly up to 1.5 million workers – to permanent repair work. Yet the potential was always greater than the achievement, and the contribution made by the bombing campaign was not decisive until it was coupled with Allied land advances. The RAF alone lost 59,223 aircrew in taking the war to Germany's heartland – it has been likened to the toll in lives in the trenches of the Western Front in World War I.

BELOW LEFT: A Republic P-47 Thunderbolt, one of the best Allied long-range fighters of the war.

RIGHT: B-17 Flying Fortresses head for Germany during a daylight mission.

BELOW RIGHT: A P-51 Mustang long-range fighter flies over England.

BELOW: Ground crew arm an American fighter with large-caliber machine-gun rounds.

CHAPTER SIX

THE BATTLE OF THE ATLANTIC

Once the German Blitzkrieg was halted at the Channel coast and the Luftwaffe had failed to win the necessary command of the air to make invasion possible, the defeat of Britain hinged largely on German capacity to blockade her by sea. The Atlantic was Britain's lifeline from the United States just as it had been during World War I when German unrestricted submarine warfare had come perilously close to starving Britain into submission; in turn, the Allies had imposed a naval blockade on German-occupied Europe that had resulted in widespread privation by 1918.

Germany had had its navy severely restricted by the Treaty of Versailles; submarines and aircraft carriers were banned and the surface fleet was limited to six heavy and six light cruisers and 24 torpedo boats. Grand Admiral Erich Raeder, who became Commander in Chief of the German Navy in 1929, wanted to build a new but balanced fleet once the opportunity offered. In 1928 the German naval staff had begun to plan for the future by exploiting a loophole in both Versailles and the subsequent Washington Naval Treaty of 1922 by building a new class of armored cruiser or pocket battleship, and the first of these, the *Deutschland*, was launched in 1929. At the same time a design bureau had been established in the Netherlands to maintain the country's expertise in submarine warfare.

Once Hitler came to power, the Navy was able to begin its construction program in earnest especially after the Anglo-German Naval Treaty of June 1935 legitimized Germany's possession of naval vessels, including submarines. In theory the Germans could now build up to 35 percent of British naval tonnage in surface vessels and up to 45 percent of British submarine tonnage. Alternatively they were entitled to build up to a total tonnage in submarines alone. However, while Rear Admiral Karl Doenitz urged construction of a submarine fleet, Raeder pressed ahead with his balanced fleet to which Hitler gave his approval in January 1939. Consequently, when the war began, the Germans had two battleships (*Scharnhorst* and *Gneisenau*), three pocket battleships (*Admiral Graf Spee*, *Deutschland*, and *Admiral Scheer*) and nine cruisers. There were just 57 submarines, of which only 20 were ocean-going craft. An aircraft carrier (*Graf Zeppelin*) had been begun but the Luftwaffe was made responsible for all air operations and it was never completed. Similarly, while other vessels were also under construction only two

PREVIOUS PAGES: *The* Scharnhorst *in icy northern waters at the beginning of the war.*

ABOVE: *The launching of the* Prinz Eugen *at Kiel on 22 August 1938.*

ABOVE RIGHT: *The pocket battleship* Deutschland *(later the Lützow) moves through the Kiel Canal in 1936, heading for open waters.*

RIGHT: *The* Graf Spee *on fire after being scuttled off Montevideo on 17 December 1939.*

LEFT: *A photograph of the* Graf Spee *in prewar review order.*

The Pocket Battleship

Officially designated *Panzerschiff* ('Armored Ship') and later as *Schwere Kreuzer* ('Heavy Cruiser'), what became popularly known as the pocket battleship was specifically designed to avoid the restrictions of the Treaty of Versailles by providing the German Navy with a vessel of a tonnage less than a cruiser but the hitting power of a battleship. Capable of resisting shells up to 8 inches, the pocket battleship could outgun anything fast enough to catch her and outrun anything heavy enough to do her damage. The first, the *Deutschland* (later renamed the *Lützow*), was launched in 1931 and like her two later sisters *Admiral Graf Spee* and *Admiral Scheer*, mounted six 27.9cm guns, eight 14.9cm guns and six 8.9cm anti-aircraft guns. She had a speed of 26 knots

and a cruising range without refueling of 12,500 miles which made her ideal for commerce raiding. Each pocket battleship cost only £3,750,000 to build. *Graf Spee*, of course, was lost in December 1939 but both *Lützow* (Hitler declined to allow any ship named after the Fatherland to be sunk by the Allies) and *Scheer* continued to pose a significant threat. Indeed, Captain Krancke of the *Admiral Scheer* conducted a brilliant solo cruise of over 46,000 miles from October 1940 to April 1941 which accounted for 17 Allied vessels including the armed merchantman *Jervis Bay* and seriously disrupted convoy planning. Eventually, *Admiral Scheer* was capsized by RAF bombs in April 1945 and the *Lützow*, which was badly damaged, scuttled a month later.

battleships (*Bismarck* and *Tirpitz*) and a cruiser (*Prinz Eugen*) were ever completed. Indeed, German naval plans had not envisaged a war until 1944 and the war began with the German Navy neither capable of meeting the Royal Navy on the high seas nor of conducting a prolonged submarine campaign.

Although the U-boats had some early successes, including the sinking of the British aircraft carrier HMS *Courageous* in September 1939 and the battleship HMS *Royal Oak* inside Scapa Flow on 14 October, the craft available could barely travel the long distance to the open Atlantic or remain on station there for more than a limited period. Consequently, German surface vessels were initially more successful as commerce raiders, and during the war German warships and the ten armed merchant raiders sank 237 Allied or neutral merchantmen. One of the armed merchantmen, the *Kormoran*, also sank HMAS *Sydney* (in November 1941) while an early victim of a German warship was the British armed merchantman *Rawalpindi*, outgunned by the *Scharnhorst* on 23 November 1939 during the latter's first wartime foray. The *Graf Spee* accounted for nine merchantmen before being caught off the River Plate in December 1939.

The loss of the *Graf Spee* was followed by other German naval losses during the Norwegian campaign. The heavy cruiser *Blücher* was torpedoed by a Norwegian coastal battery, the light cruiser *Königsberg* was sunk by British aircraft and the light cruiser *Karlsruhe* was sunk by a British submarine. German destroyers were also worsted off Narvik by a Royal Navy force including the battleship HMS *Warspite*. However, the Luftwaffe was displaying the power of aircraft against naval targets by inflicting serious damage on British ships, while *Scharnhorst* and *Gneisenau* sank the aircraft carrier HMS *Glorious*, and the cruiser *Admiral Hipper* sank the British destroyer HMS *Glowworm* while it was covering mine-laying operations on 8 April 1940.

The German Navy had thus suffered heavily in Norwegian waters and damage to the *Scharnhorst* and *Gneisenau* reduced it to one cruiser and four destroyers fit for sea by June 1940. However, the successes of the German Army in western Europe opened up new possibilities for submarine warfare as French and Norwegian ports became available. The distance to the Atlantic was shortened and, in the case of the French ports, there was no

LEFT: The Hipper *in dry-dock for repairs after its brief engagement with HMS* Glowworm *in April 1940.*

BELOW LEFT: An Atlantic convoy heads out into the north Atlantic. A British destroyer provides a degree of protection from surface raiders and U-boats.

Mines

Another naval weapon which saw considerable development during the war was the mine. Although the magnetic mine was first introduced in 1918, the model developed by the Germans was of unknown polarity in 1939. Consequently, when one which fell at Shoeburyness in November 1939 was recovered intact by Lieutenant Commander J G D Ouvry, it enabled the British to reduce ships' magnetic field – degaussing – to counter the impact of the device. In order to sweep magnetic mines already sown, however, it was necessary to devise a new method of towing electric cables of predetermined length on the surface which produced a magnetic field strong enough to set off the mines without harm to the minesweeper.

Another German mine was acoustic and capable of acting on the noise of a ship passing overhead. This was countered by an electric-powered hammer in a ship's bows striking the hull and creating sufficient noise to explode the mine well ahead of the ship. More conventional sweeping was undertaken with a cable towed between minesweeper and a 'paravane' cutting mine cables and bringing the mines to the surface where they could be detonated by rifle fire.

The Allies also sowed mines as well as sweeping them and large barriers of mines were used to close off areas such as the Straits of Dover or to inhibit the exit routes of U-boats to the Atlantic off the Norwegian coast. Indeed, British-laid minefields off Norway disposed of three U-boats and others were destroyed by magnetic mines sown by the British ships in the Baltic.

necessity to negotiate the North Sea or the Straits of Dover. More U-boats could also be kept on station for longer periods and from headquarters at Lorient in Brittany, Doenitz organized the first 'wolfpacks' – a large number of submarines that could be assembled rapidly around a convoy. Another menace to shipping was the long-range Focke Wulf Condor bomber which also operated from Norway and France. Indeed, in early 1941 these airplanes were matching the U-boats in terms of numbers of ships sunk.

When the war had begun the Royal Navy had had only 87 escort ships of which only 27 were initially available in the western approaches. They also had a short range of only 500 miles and, where they were assigned to convoys, they were often overwhelmed by the sheer number of submarines with which they had to deal in running battles that could last for several days. The Admiralty had decided in 1937 to institute convoys if it appeared that the Germans were waging unrestricted submarine warfare, and with the sinking of the liner *Athenia* on 3 September 1939 a convoy system was introduced.

Not only was there a lack of escorts generally but the technical means available – ASDIC and depth charges – were no longer adequate to deal with modern submarines. Both ASDIC, which took its name from the Allied Submarine Detection and Investigation Committee of 1917, and depth charges dated from World War I. ASDIC had a minimum range as well as a maximum and an escort would lose track of its target when going into an attack. Similarly, the depth charges were designed to detonate at too shallow a depth to damage modern deep-running submarines. In any case, neither ASDIC nor depth charges could cope with a submarine attacking on the surface at night, which was the favored U-boat tactic at this stage of the war. It was recognized that aircraft would play a major role in keeping submarines submerged and therefore slower and more vulnerable but there were no aircraft yet available with sufficient range to cover the mid-Atlantic. In 1939 a total of 95 Allied and neutral merchant ships were lost and just nine U-boats, while in 1940, the Germans sank 822 merchantmen for the loss of only 22 U-boats. Despite increasing American involvement in the naval war in the Atlantic another 1141 merchantmen went to the bottom during 1941 and only 35 U-boats.

TOP RIGHT: Admiral Doenitz (right) greets one of his successful U-boat crews on completion of a patrol in the North Sea.

CENTER RIGHT: Reloading depth charges on the Royal Navy corvette HMS Dianthus *in 1942.*

RIGHT: A merchantman settles into the water after an attack by a U-boat on 9 June 1941.

LEFT: Lookouts on a U-boat scan the horizon for potential victims or Allied long-range anti-submarine aircraft.

LEFT: Loading torpedoes on the U-124 in March 1941.

BELOW: An armed merchantman fitted with a catapult-launched Hurricane protects the ships of a North Atlantic convoy.

ABOVE: The U-101 coming alongside a supply ship in mid-Atlantic.

LEFT: A U-boat gun crew prepares to open fire on the merchantman seen in the distance.

BELOW: Returning from a successful cruise. For many crews, however, the war ended in a watery grave.

LEFT: *The aircraft carrier* HMS Ark Royal *sinking on 10 November 1941 after a submarine attack.*

TOP RIGHT: *The* Bismarck *firing a salvo at HMS* Hood *in the Denmark Strait on 24 May 1941.*

CENTER RIGHT: *A salvo from* Bismarck *straddles HMS* Rodney.

BELOW RIGHT: *Survivors of the* Bismarck *are brought aboard HMS* Dorsetshire *after the sinking of their vessel.*

BELOW: *An Italian battleship fires a full broadside during a training exercise in the Mediterranean.*

The fall of France had also had repercussions on the naval balance in the Mediterranean. The world's fourth largest fleet – that of France – was effectively lost to the western Allies even if it did not fall into German hands. At the same time, the Italian Navy entered the fray with a fleet of fast modern battleships. However, the daring attack on Taranto by 20 elderly Swordfish aircraft from HMS *Illustrious* on the night of 10 November 1940 crippled three Italian battleships, half the Italian capital strength, for the loss of only two airplanes. Unfortunately, *Illustrious* was then badly damaged on 13 January 1941 by the aircraft of the Luftwaffe's Fliegerkorps X dispatched to Sicily by Hitler to assist the Italians. It was this force that also subjected Malta to sustained aerial bombardment, although Swordfish squadrons operating from the island accounted for a monthly average of 50,000 tons of Axis shipping between 1941 and 1943 and played an enormous part in disrupting Rommel's supply chain. The Royal Navy also struck a further blow when information derived from ULTRA enabled Admiral Sir Andrew Cunningham's Mediterranean Fleet to catch an Italian naval force heading to cut off the British reinforcement of Greece. On 26 March 1941 three Italian cruisers and two destroyers were sunk off Cape Matapan and the battleship *Vittorio Veneto* was also crippled. Only one Swordfish from the carrier HMS *Formidable* was lost but the Royal Navy itself then suffered grievous losses to German aircraft off Crete. Three cruisers and six destroyers were sunk and a further 17 ships including three battleships damaged.

The Royal Navy's success in disrupting supplies to Rommel also led Hitler to divert Fliegerkorps II from Russia and U-boats from the Atlantic into the Mediterranean. As a result the carrier HMS *Ark Royal*, the battleship HMS *Barham* and the cruiser HMS *Galatea* were all lost to torpedoes on 10 November, 25 November, and 14 December 1941 respectively. On 19 December Italian frogmen also managed to damage the battleships *Valiant* and *Queen Elizabeth* in Alexandria harbor, but their nine attacks on shipping at Gibraltar between September 1940 and August 1943 were far less successful. With severely reduced resources, Cunningham attempted to keep Malta supplied through convoys such as *Excess* (January 1941), *Substance* (July 1941), *Halberd* (September 1941), and *Harpoon* and *Vigorous* (June 1942). The latter two convoys, which were started simultaneously from Alexandria and Gibraltar lost 15 out of 17 merchantmen despite an escort of 82 warships. However, despite the loss of the carrier HMS *Eagle* and the crippling of the carrier *Indomitable*, the *Pedestal* convoy in August 1942 succeeded in getting three out of 13 merchantmen and the damaged tanker *Ohio* into Malta with enough supplies to sustain the island until December. Further convoys in November and December 1942 then ensured Malta could survive until the spring of 1943, by which time the Eighth Army had driven Rommel back to Tunisia.

British naval difficulties in the Mediterranean were reflected in the Atlantic since it reduced available escorts still further. In 1941 the Germans launched both the cruiser *Prinz Eugen* and the battleship *Bismarck*. In May the two vessels were dispatched commerce raiding. In the Denmark Strait on 24 May 1941 they met the British battleship HMS *Hood* in the company of the new battleship HMS *Prince of Wales* and six destroyers. Within just eight minutes of the action opening, the *Hood* had been blown to pieces by *Bismarck*'s fifth salvo for the loss of all but three of her crew of 1419 officers and men. The *Prince of Wales* was also hit but managed to start an oil leak on the *Bismarck* which compelled the German ship to run for Brest for repairs. Intercepted radio messages relocated the *Bismarck* after she had eluded the *Prince of Wales* and Swordfish from HMS *Ark Royal* attacked her on 26 May, a torpedo jamming the *Bismarck*'s rudder so that she could only steer in circles. The battleships HMS *King George V*

and HMS *Rodney* pounded the crippled ship and the cruiser HMS *Dorsetshire* then sank her with torpedoes at 1040 on 27 May. The *Prinz Eugen* had slipped away on 24 May and reached the safety of Brest on 1 June to join the *Scharnhorst* and *Gneisenau*, which had returned there from raiding into the Atlantic in March.

In reality, Brest was something of an uncertain refuge since it could be easily blockaded by the Royal Navy and was in range of RAF bombers – both *Scharnhorst* and *Gneisenau* were hit in raids. However, Raeder was reluctant to risk the ships in the open sea and they only emerged in January 1942 when Hitler demanded that they return to German waters or be decommissioned. The British were aware of the imminent departure of *Scharnhorst*, *Gneisenau*, and *Prinz Eugen* but, through a series of unfortunate gaps in British air patrols, their sailing on the night of 11 February was missed and the ships were 13 hours and 300 miles up the Channel before being detected. Six Swordfish led by Lieutenant Commander Eugene Esmonde launched a torpedo attack but all were lost together with 13 of the 18 aircrew, and RAF bombers also failed to stop the German ships. Although *Scharnhorst* hit a mine all three ships reached home waters. In the event, the return of the ships to the north posed no immediate threat and within a fortnight *Prinz Eugen* had been damaged by a torpedo and the *Gneisenau* crippled by RAF bombing. However, the 'Channel Dash' was certainly a grave embarrassment to the Royal Navy.

Yet another naval 'front' was opened when the Germans invaded Russia since the British resolved to send supplies by convoy through the Arctic to Murmansk, the first of the PQ series sailing on 28 September 1941. Battling through the most appalling weather, the Arctic convoys were under constant threat from German submarines, aircraft, and surface ships based in Norway. In fact, *Prinz*

Eugen was damaged en route to Norwegian waters in order to threaten the British convoys. The escorts were capable of dealing with German submarines and airplanes but not attack from capital ships. Thus, when the newly completed battleship *Tirpitz* was thought to be heading for Convoy *PQ-17* in July 1942 the convoy was ordered to scatter. Without the protection of escorts, the isolated merchantmen were easy targets and 21 were lost in five days. As a result Churchill suspended the convoys until the fall since longer Arctic nights would then offer greater security. Once the convoys were revived, the Germans attempted to reproduce their earlier success by attacking Convoy *JW-51B* on 31 December 1942 with a force including the pocket battleship *Lützow* (formerly the *Deutschland*) and the cruiser *Admiral Hipper*. The Royal Navy destroyer escort accompanying the convoy through the Barents Sea managed to keep the German ships at bay with the threat of torpedo attack and also damaged the *Hipper*. Hitler was so incensed that he ordered the battle fleet scrapped. Raeder resigned as Commander in Chief in protest and was replaced by Doenitz. Doenitz managed to persuade Hitler to retain both *Scharnhorst* and *Tirpitz* while the others were decommissioned or turned into training ships or floating batteries. However, even the presence of just the two battleships and the *Lützow* in northern waters was sufficient to fulfill the role of 'fleet in being' and persuade Churchill once more to suspend Arctic convoys for the summer months.

Nevertheless, naval operations by the Germans were thereafter limited. When the *Scharnhorst* emerged to attack Convoy *JW-55B* off the North Cape on 26 December 1943 the British were waiting with a force that included the battleship HMS *Duke of York*. Her gunfire and torpedoes from accompanying cruisers and destroyers sank the *Scharnhorst*. The *Tirpitz* still remained a

ABOVE: *The* Tirpitz *camouflaged in Flehke Fjord, Norway. This sister to the* Bismarck *remained a threat in being to Allied vessels for much of the war.*

TOP RIGHT: *The end of the* Tirpitz *in Trömso Fjord, Norway, after a heavy bombing raid in November 1944.*

ABOVE RIGHT: *Escorting German E-boats and aircraft photographed from the* Prinz Eugen *during the Channel Dash of the* Scharnhorst *and* Gneisenau, *13 February 1942.*

RIGHT: *A Royal Navy X-craft underway; such mini-subs carried out a successful raid against the* Tirpitz *in a Norwegian fjord.*

threat. The first of many attempts to sink her with bombs had been made in January 1942 while the British had also raided St Nazaire to destroy the 'Normandie' dock in March 1942 since it was the only installation in France large enough to accommodate the battleship. Attempts to sink the *Tirpitz* were also made by chariots ('human' torpedoes) in October 1942 and by miniature X-craft submarines in September 1943, the latter causing some damage. *Tirpitz* was finally sunk on 12 November 1944 by the RAF using 12,000-lb 'blockbuster' armor-piercing bombs in Tromsö Fjord. In fact, although supplies were also channeled to the Soviet Union around the Cape of Good Hope and through the Persian Gulf and, after American entry to the war, across the Pacific to Vladivostock, the volume of materiel transported did not reach the Soviets in really large quantities until 1943 when they had already weathered the storm.

Formal United States entry into the war in December 1941 also brought a switch in the focus of the German submarine campaign. Doenitz resolved to avoid larger concentrations of Allied warships by attacking shipping in transit between the United States and Latin America, whence the Americans derived much of their raw material. Hitler endorsed Operation *Paukenschlag* ('Roll the Drums') on 12 December 1941 and although only five U-boats could be spared they sank 87 merchantmen in four months. Truly it was the 'Happy Time' for the U-boats. Even more might have been achieved if Hitler had not chosen to send 50 submarines to the Mediterranean. These undoubtedly contributed to the Royal Navy's difficulties as has already been indicated but they would have done far more damage in the Atlantic. As it was, the sight of merchantmen sinking off American beaches caused considerable disquiet in the United States and accelerated the search for a new model escort vessel. So-called Destroyer Escorts were put into production although they had a lower priority than amphibious landing craft for Operation Torch and there were still only 25 in commission by June 1943.

Difficulties were also encountered in co-ordinating efforts by the US Navy and the US Army Air Force to improve air cover. The real solution was to build small escort carriers on merchant ship hulls. An early version appeared in December 1941 with Convoy *HG76* from Gibraltar and proved its worth when five U-boats were destroyed and only two merchantmen. The first of the new-style escort carriers operating in properly constituted escort groups was the USS *Bogue* which sailed for the first time with Convoy *SC123* in March 1943. Eventually, there were 116 escort carriers with the US Navy and 25 with the Royal Navy, usually capable of carrying between 15 and 24 airplanes. The threat from the Condor bombers was also met by improvising catapult-fitted Merchantships (CAM), from which a Hurricane could be catapulted into flight and subsequently recovered from the sea. Eventually, too, longer-range aircraft became available, such as the Liberator which enabled air cover from land-based aircraft to be provided over virtually the entire North Atlantic route. RAF Coastal Command also carried out a sustained aerial offensive against U-boat transit routes to the Atlantic utilizing technological developments such as aerial depth charges and, from 1943, airborne homing depth charges. Despite this strategy Doenitz's U-boats continued to enjoy considerable success. In 1942 another 1570 merchant ships were sunk and 86 U-boats, but the Germans were building new submarines at a rate of one a day and Doenitz was able to keep an average of 75 U-boats at sea through 1942.

It was only during 1943 that the tide slowly turned in the battle for the Atlantic routes. As early as May 1941 the British had captured a U-boat's Enigma machine and soon broken the German cipher. The Germans changed the code in early 1942 and it was not until December 1942 that the Allies deciphered it. This revealed that the Germans had penetrated the British convoy codes and when these were changed in mid-1943 it damaged German convoy intelligence considerably. Equally important, however, were the technical developments on the Allied side. In late 1941 the contact-fused, multi-barreled 'Hedgehog' mortar had been introduced to enable escorts to fire ahead of themselves while still maintaining ASDIC contact with submarines. By 1944 a still better weapon became available in the form of the 'Squid,' which enabled a pattern of depth charges to be thrown which could damage a submarine by detonation without coming into contact with the U-boat hull. High-frequency direction finding had been introduced in 1942, helping escorts to chase their quarry along any bearing obtained, and in the following year a better ASDIC became available which could gauge depth accurately. The greatest development was radar, which was first introduced in a primitive fashion in September 1940 but improved enormously thereafter. By March 1941 an escort with radar could already locate a fully surfaced submarine at 5000 yards, a partially submerged submarine at 2800 yards and a periscope at 1300 yards. In March 1943 the Washington Convoy Conference evolved a scheme for dividing the Atlantic into zones of responsibility with the Royal and Canadian Navies handling the North Atlantic routes and the US Navy, which had to find escorts for both the Pacific and convoys to North Africa, taking on the less busy Central Atlantic routes. The Americans also continued to administer the Interlocking Convoy system introduced in 1942 to match eastward bound convoys to escorts in the manner of a railway timetable.

The turning point came in April and May 1943, when Convoy *ONS5* survived the attack of 60 U-boats, losing only 12 merchantmen while the escorts accounted for six submarines. The figures for the two months as a whole showed 56 U-boats sunk and only 92 merchantmen. The

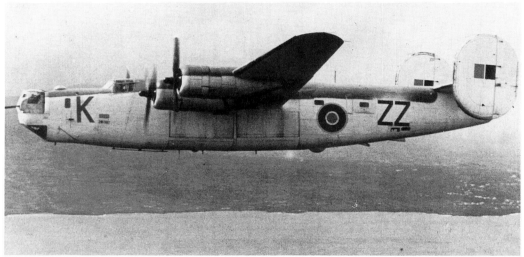

losses drove the U-boats from the Atlantic for three months and they never returned in the same strength again. Doenitz had calculated that if he could sink Allied tonnage faster than it could be replaced then he would prevail, but by July 1943 the Allies were more than matching losses with new ship construction. The Germans themselves attempted to restore the balance with their own technical developments. The schnorkel, which was actually a Dutch invention, enabled a submarine to run underwater on its diesel engines rather than on storage

ABOVE: An RAF Short Sunderland flying boat on convoy duty.

batteries; the new XXI U-boat developed in 1944 offered better underwater speed through improved shape and a double hull incorporating additional battery capacity, although it did not see its first voyage until April 1945. An experimental steam turbine was also not developed in time although the Germans did experiment successfully with new torpedoes. One model was the forerunner of modern acoustic homing devices and another was capable of changing course to a predetermined pattern to search for merchant ships; but it was all too late.

In June 1944 the Allied landings in Normandy spelled the end of the French U-boat bases and four months later Portugal agreed to Allied air bases being constructed on the Azores, which ensured that land-based aircraft could now cover mid-ocean routes. In 1943 U-boat losses had totaled 237 to 597 merchantmen and in 1944 the Allies sunk another 241 U-boats compared to the loss of 205 merchantmen. In the last five months of the war another 153 U-boats were lost and only 97 merchantmen. Of the remaining German submarine force, 215 U-boats were scuttled and 154 fell into Allied hands.

Convoy Defense

Instituting a convoy system for the protection of merchantmen in wartime was a method well known to the age of sail before it was resurrected during World War I. Success in protecting troop transports and the coastal coal trade by convoy persuaded the British Admiralty, albeit reluctantly, to begin a convoy system in May 1917. It was a natural weapon, therefore, to re-introduce in 1939. However, due to the limited number of escort vessels available it was not until 1942 that convoys became more effective in the battle against the U-boats.

The first real indication of increasing efficiency was Convoy *HG76* from Gibraltar to Britain in December 1941. It was not only notable for the use of an escort carrier for the first time but also for the tactics employed by the convoy commander, Captain F J ('Johnnie') Walker. Walker, who was to become the most resourceful of submarine hunters with 44 U-boats accounted for by vessels under his direction, was prepared to deliberately weaken the perimeter screen by leaving it to hunt down submarine contacts. He also developed 'plaster attacks' with one vessel holding ASDIC contact with a U-boat and directing others to the course of the submarine. These other escorts would then cross the U-boat course at slow speeds depth-charging to the side or front to counter any evasive action by the submarine, which would be unaware of their presence because of an increase in pro-

peller noise usually concomitant with a surging escort attack. Once even more escorts became available in the Atlantic, groups leaving the convoy to take aggressive action against U-boats became commonplace but Walker had done so when escorts were still numerically weak. Another of his ploys was to counter German acoustic torpedoes by exceptionally low or high speeds or by dropping depth charges to detonate the torpedoes.

Adding to the effectiveness of convoy defense was constant scientific and operational research. Professor P M S Blackett made the important calculation at the end of 1942 that the number of ships in a convoy could be substantially increased without greater loss since it increased the area relative to the perimeter by an increase in radius with an optimum number of escorts (nine) for its defense. This freed other escorts for hunting groups. Another factor was the steady evolution in the escorts themselves. At the start of the war, the Admiralty ordered a design based on a whale-catcher known as the Flower class corvettes. Some 56 were built and though hardy in bad weather, they lacked sufficient speed and the space for new weaponry. They were replaced by the Castle class corvettes and then by the River class frigates which could outpace a U-boat on the surface. In turn, the Loch and Bay class frigates gave substantially better performances as did later Black Swan class sloops.

TOP LEFT: *A Mosquito of RAF Coastal Command attacking a German U-boat.*

CENTER LEFT: *A longe-range Liberator of RAF Coastal Command's No 120 Squadron patrols over the Azores in search of enemy submarines.*

ABOVE: *A 'Hedgehog' battery on a Royal Navy destroyer.*

RIGHT: *An armed merchantman, SS* Coulmore, *riding out an Atlantic storm in 1943.*

HITLERS' BOMBS
CANT BEAT US
OUR ORANGES
CAME THROUGH
MUSSOS 'LAKE'

CHAPTER SEVEN

CIVILIANS AT WAR

It is now widely accepted that war has often played an important role in historical development. In particular, the concept of 'total war' has become a familiar way of describing World Wars I and II. The term was apparently first used by General Erich Ludendorff in 1919 but it was ritually employed during World War II. Goebbels, for example, threated the Allies with 'total war' in a speech of February 1943 and was appointed Reich Plenipotentiary for the Mobilization of Total War in July 1944. Churchill also used the phrase in an address to the US Congress in May 1943. Since 1945, the idea has become synonymous with war as a catalyst for far-reaching social change.

This is not to suggest that earlier wars were not profound in their effects, only that warfare had become increasingly more 'total' in its impact. Of course, both 'world' wars were just what that phrase implies, being far greater in scale than any earlier conflict. In the case of World War II, it began as purely a European conflict but widened progressively with the aggression of Germany, Italy, and Japan. Successive German and Soviet occupations led to a bewildering proliferation of contradictory declarations of war in eastern Europe, and between February and March 1945 no less than ten states, ranging from Saudi Arabia to Peru, hastened to declare war on both Germany and Japan and a further two states on Japan alone.

Total war also implied that the scale of destruction would be greater than ever before. While World War II did not witness the use of poison gas, other than in the context of Nazi genocide, its military use was suggested by a powerful lobby in Germany. Technological advances brought far greater capacity to kill, Germany introduced the V-weapons in 1944 and the Allies ended the war with the atomic bomb. The aims of the belligerents were also more far-reaching, with Germany pursuing world domination and the western Allies adopting a declaration at the Casablanca Conference in January 1943 which demanded Germany's unconditional surrender. Similarly, at the Cairo Conference in December of the same year, Britain and the United States were joined by the Nationalist Chinese in agreeing to strip Japan of all those overseas

PREVIOUS PAGES: Business as usual in London's East End during the Blitz, September 1940.

ABOVE: Londoners shelter in the Elephant and Castle underground station during the Blitz.

TOP RIGHT: The village school at Petworth in West Sussex after being hit by a lone German bomber in 1941.

LEFT: Fires rage in Coventry, November 1940.

RIGHT: Japanese children practise air-raid precautions during the height of the US strategic bomber offensive.

territories she had taken by force of arms since 1894. Both Germany and Japan faced major political, social, and economic restructuring after defeat, but then those countries occupied by the Germans and Japanese had faced equal changes. Wider aims were also sold to the people of the belligerent states by sustained propaganda campaigns, the war of words and images being as much a contribution to victory or defeat as any other aspect of the conflict.

With such determination added to such enhanced capacity to destroy, the loss of life and property dwarfed all previous wars. World War II may have cost the lives of 30 million people in Europe alone although some put Soviet losses at over 20 million. The figures include an estimated 5.9 million Jewish victims of the Nazis while another 26 million people may have been displaced from their countries of origin. At least a million Poles were displaced, and foreign laborers brought to Germany reached a peak of seven million in 1944. Then there were the prisoners of war. Of some five million Soviet citizens captured by Germany and her Allies, at least two million died in captivity and another million were never accounted for. Even in Britain, which did not suffer invasion or conquest, there were 60 million changes of address during the war. These figures for dead or displaced are mainly those of civilians rather than soldiers, sailors, or airmen. Indeed, in total war the civilian was a legitimate target. German civilian losses to Allied bombing may have been 593,000, but the fire raids on Tokyo killed 83,000 people in a single night in March 1945, about the same number of immediate deaths at Hiroshima and Nagasaki combined five months later. Nevertheless, it must be said that war on

LEFT: *A wartime factory concert in Berlin, 8 June 1943.*

BELOW: *Soviet workers assembling heavy anti-aircraft guns in a plant in the Urals. After the German invasion of 1941, much of Russia's industrial plant was moved eastward to avoid capture.*

BELOW RIGHT: *A female foreign laborer in a German factory, 20 June 1944.*

such a scale also brought enormous medical advances, McIndoe's pioneering plastic surgery being but one.

Losses in terms of property or manufacturing and agricultural production were equally enormous although it is difficult to arrive at a meaningful figure. Germany, for example, has been calculated as having lost 212,000 buildings to Allied bombing and the Soviet Union 3.5 million dwellings to German military activity. Statistics hardly convey the reality of destruction. Certainly, European manufacturing suffered greatly and had to be rebuilt after the war in many cases but non-European economies such as that of the United States benefited from the war. The blow struck at Europe not only led to economic decline, at least in the short term, but also to political decline vis-à-vis the rise of the United States and the Soviet Union as global superpowers.

Above all, Japanese successes in Southeast Asia in 1941 and 1942 dealt a blow to European colonial prestige from which it never recovered. Asian nationalism was fostered both through the establishment by the Japanese of puppet governments with a limited degree of autonomy and also through the appearance of anti-Japanese movements such as the Viet Minh in French Indochina, the Hukbalahap in the Philippines, and the Malayan People's Anti-Japanese Army. Subsequently, these movements – largely led by communists – were to resist the return of the European colonial authorities. In the course of the war, Britain was forced to concede a promise for Indian independence, and both African and Asian servicemen engaged in what was proclaimed to be a war for freedom could hardly fail to become imbued with some degree of desire for their own feedom. At the same time, the war saw the resurgence of the attempt to create an international mechanism for world order. The United Nations was born in the Atlantic Charter meeting between Churchill and Roosevelt in August 1941, and was effectively created at the conference held at the Dumbarton Oaks estate near Washington between August and October 1944.

In most countries, the war also increased the power of the state over the individual. Even in Britain there was an enormous growth in bureaucracy with new ministries of supply, home security, food, shipping, economic warfare, information, and aircraft production, created in 1939 and 1940. In the United States there were departments such as the War Production Board, Office of Price Administration, and National War Labor Board, with the number of state employees increasing from a million in 1940 to 3.8 million by 1946. In some countries such as the Soviet Union and Nazi Germany there was already a significant degree of state coercion. In 1941 all Soviet workers in war industries and transport were rendered subject to military discipline, and in the following year overtime became compulsory. In Germany all changes of employment were prohibited in June 1942 unless authorized, and in January 1943 all males between 16 and 65 and all females between 17 and 45 were required to register for work of national importance.

In countries that fell under foreign domination, the

BELOW: ATS girls manning the range-finder of an anti-aircraft battery. With a large part of the male population at the front, women were able to move into many key areas of the war economy of Britain.

German Occupation Policies

Hitler's immediate aim in 1939 was victory and not the re-ordering of Europe in the fashion of the Nazi 'New Order.' As a result, roles were assigned to newly conquered territories which would least interfere with the further prosecution of the war. Occasionally areas were annexed outright such as the Polish Corridor but others were subjected only to indirect rule, including Denmark where the government was allowed to function until 1943, and the various puppet states such as Slovakia and Croatia. Even direct German rule could vary, with Belgium and occupied France under a military administration but the Netherlands under civil German administration, and 'non-Germanic' areas given over to agencies such as the SS and Hans Frank's Central Government in Poland. The SS and Alfred Rosenberg's Ministry for Occupied Eastern Territories were made responsible for clearing the east of its inhabitants and encouraging German colonization and Germanization. Certain groups were judged suitable for absorption into the German *Herrenvolk* and their children frequently abducted for adoption in Germany where they could be molded into the ways of the master race. Alongside the racial policies were those for economic exploitation which could again vary from stripping raw materials to extracting production through occupation agreements or imposing crippling financial reparations and assessments for supporting the forces of occupation and then utilizing the surplus credit to buy up raw materials.

treatment accorded the people could vary enormously. In the case of Germany; for example, Alsace-Lorraine in France and parts of Belgium were fully integrated into the Reich but others such as Moravia and Bohemia – parts of Czechoslovakia – were regarded as protectorates within a greater Germany while Slovakia got its own puppet administration. Denmark and the Netherlands were treated largely as if they were potential allies, but by contrast Poland and occupied parts of the Soviet Union were subjected to the most ruthless exploitation.

Such disparities conditioned the degree of co-operation or resistance encountered, for every individual was confronted by a choice as to his or her reaction to defeat and occupation. There were nationalists who chose to fight a hated foreign occupation but, equally, there were those in countries such as the Netherlands or Norway who saw the Soviet Union as a greater enemy than Germany. The Waffen SS recruited 'legions' from most occupied countries and, despite the brutality of their occupation, the Germans also drew large numbers of recruits from Russian minorities. The Japanese equivalents were Aung San's Burma National Army and Subhas Chandra Bose's Indian National Army.

The intensity of resistance could also vary. Obviously, open guerrilla warfare was an impossibility in a low-lying country like Denmark and was far more suited to mountainous terrain as in Greece and Yugoslavia. In any case, it might embrace a variety of unseen gestures – perhaps listening to the BBC or reading a clandestine newspaper – just as much as hiding Allied airmen, Jews, or those liable to deportation as foreign labor. Then again, some groups chose to concentrate on gathering intelligence or preferred to wait like the *Milorg* in Norway for the very eve of liberation. Passive resistance was also a legitimate response. Norwegian schoolteachers staged an effective strike in protest against a new fascist-orientated school syllabus introduced by the collaborationist government of Vidkun Quisling, whose very name came to represent collaboration. And of course resistance also meant direct action varying from sabotage to partisan warfare.

On occasions, sabotage could be spectacularly successful as in the destruction of the Gorgopotamos Viaduct in Greece in 1942 or the attack on the German heavy-water plant to Vemork in Norway in February 1943 and the destruction of Germany's remaining stocks of heavy water aboard the Tinnso ferry in Norway in February 1944. Rarely, however, was sabotage lastingly successful and attempts at open insurrection such as the rising in the Warsaw Ghetto in April 1943, the rising of the Polish Home Army in the same city in August 1944, and the French *maquis*' attempt to establish liberated zones in Savoy in March 1944 and at Vercours near Grenoble three months later, could prove disastrous. Reprisals that followed resistance activity could also result in savagery as when the Nazis eliminated over 2000 Czechs in the village of Lidice in June 1942 following the assassination of Heydrich, Himmler's deputy, or the massacre by the Waffen SS of the inhabitants of Oradour-sur-Glane in France in June 1944 after the *Das Reich* Division had been held up by partisans en route to the Normandy beachhead. An estimated 30,000 French men and women died in German reprisals during the war while in Poland it was standard practice to shoot ten Poles for every German killed.

Nevertheless, resistance could help; the sabotage inflicted on German transportation and communications by the French *maquis* mentioned above were especially effective in combination with Allied air attacks. But above all resistance did much for the morale of those under occupation for four years or more. It also resulted in what might be termed upward social mobility since resistance was invariably reformist in character and brought new elites into prominence after the war that had had no share in government prior to 1939. In some cases a social and political

revolution was forged through resistance. In Yugoslavia Tito created the fabric of a postwar socialist state through political action hand-in-hand with military action. Communist guerrillas were also active in Italy and Greece, although they failed to achieve power, and the same was true in Southeast Asian countries. Here too the war most certainly assisted the Chinese communists since Chiang Kai-shek's Nationalists were too busy fighting the Japanese to eliminate Mao Tse-tung's communist forces, although the three-cornered fight in China had been going on since 1937 and the war between Chiang and the communists since 1927.

Prisoners of war and internees also suffered coercion. Those Allied soldiers who fell into the hands of the Japanese were especially unfortunate, over 12,000 alone dying on the notorious Burma-Siam railway. But the fate of Soviet prisoners in German hands and vice versa was also dire. Nor was coercion of this kind confined to the Axis and totalitarian states. In the United States 100,000

SOE and OSS

Much of the Allied assistance of European and Far Eastern resistance groups was channeled through the British Special Operations Executive (SOE) and United States Office of Strategic Services (OSS). SOE was formed in July 1940 to co-ordinate sabotage and subversion in occupied Europe, formal responsibility being vested in the minister of economic warfare. In practice however SOE operated beyond executive control in many instances, enjoying poor relations with other parts of the British secret services and bedeviled by the kind of rivalries and intrigues that tended to proliferate in the world of secrets. Rather similarly, OSS clashed with the Federal Bureau of Investigation (FBI), which jealously guarded its supposed priority in Latin America, and with MacArthur in the Pacific who wanted to run his own organization independent of OSS. Nor were relations between SOE and OSS all they might have been, notably in Greece, and the groups each chose to back in particular countries often had a distinct bearing on the postwar political make up of the states concerned. SOE appears to have attained a strength of some 13,000 men and women by 1944 and OSS a similar number.

ABOVE LEFT: Nazi Brownshirts parade through the streets of Danzig after its capture in September 1939.

CENTER LEFT: SS guards in front of one of Prague's main buildings in occupied Czechoslovakia.

RIGHT: Members of the French Forces of the Interior (FFI) in Normandy after liberation. Partisans were, if organized, able to tie down large numbers of the German occupation forces.

LEFT: A German soldier captured by FFI personnel during street fighting in Paris on the eve of the French capital's liberation.

RIGHT: German retaliation for attacks on their troops in occupied Russia – hanged partisans. Atrocities on a large scale were the hallmark of the Nazi treatment of subjugated peoples.

LEFT: The remains of a German artillery battery ambushed by Yugoslav partisans north of Sarajevo in April 1945.

RIGHT: Tito (right), the Yugoslavian partisan leader, with his chief of staff, General Yovanovitch.

BELOW: Stuart light tanks – some of the increasing war material supplied to Tito's partisans toward the end of the war.

BELOW RIGHT: Czech rebels during the Slovak Rising in Prague.

citizens of Japanese origin were forcibly removed from the Pacific coast between March and June 1942 to 'relocation centers' and they were not permitted to return to their homes until January 1945.

Coercion of one kind or another was just as much a feature of western democracies in total war as of other states. The British government took enormously wide powers under the Emergency Powers (Defense) Act of September 1939 and its revised version in May 1940. In reality, there were few compulsory labor directions, and although Britain went further than any other belligerent in taking powers for the conscription of women the legislation was used sparingly. However, there was compulsory direction of men to the mining industry – the so-called 'Bevin Boys,' – in 1943, and following a spate of unofficial strikes it became an indictable offense in April 1944 to instigate or incite stoppages in essential war industries. Canada compulsorily transferred 127,000 workers from low- to high-priority industry in January 1943, and the War Labor Disputes Act in the United States in the same year also enabled government to conscript strikers. At a lower level there were the innumerable restrictions such as the black-out imposed in Britain in September 1939, rationing of commodities such as butter, bacon, and sugar and the introduction of double summer time, summer time itself being a product of World War I.

In many cases, the powers taken and used were to ensure the control of the economy and a fundamental concept in total war was that the state must utilize every

resource available to it in order to survive. In effect, total war meant total mobilization. There is a lively debate about whether Germany ever managed to create this kind of total war economy. An earlier interpretation suggested that the German economy was designed only for Blitzkrieg prior to 1942, so that there was little in-depth defense capacity and a major effort was required by Albert Speer as armaments minister to convert to a war economy. By contrast, others have argued more recently that fewer changes were required since Germany had been creating a war economy since 1936 despite the competing agencies and vested interests that resulted in gross inefficiency prior to the war. Thus, Speer's efforts were an attempt to improve the performance of an economy already geared for total war. Certainly, the pace quickened after 1942 and Speer was able to increase production significantly notwithstanding escalation of the Allied strategic bombing campaign against German industry.

The introduction of a total war economy inevitably demanded the full mobilization of manpower and the direction of that manpower to essential industries as well as to the armed forces. In Canada, for example, the shipbuilding industry increased the size of its workforce from 4000 in 1939 to 126,000 by 1943 and the United States labor force increased from 54 million to 64 million. The numbers of women in employment also increased dramatically in order to release men for other tasks. In Britain there were three million more women in full- or part-time employment in 1943 than in 1939 and in the United States 4.5 million more in 1945 than in 1940. In the Soviet Union 51 percent of all industrial workers and 71 percent of all agricultural workers were women by 1945. A parallel can be drawn with another disadvantaged group in the United States, the number of black people in employment increased from 2.9 million in 1940 to 3.2 million by 1944.

Certain sectors of industry received a particular stimulus, notably heavy industries such as coal, shipping, and heavy metals; but newer industries such as chemicals, electricals, and motors also benefited. In the United States there was a boom in synthetic rubber manufacture due to the loss of Southeast Asian rubber supplies with Japanese occupation. Such industrial development generally meant declining unemployment and enhanced bargaining power for labor. Trade union membership invariably increased and, generally speaking, resulted in shorter working hours and higher wages in real terms. These changes were possible because governmental need to ensure better relations with labor increased union strength and continued militancy had an increasing impact on industrial relations. However, averages do not always reflect reality and there were wide differences between industries and within industries. In Britain industrial wage differentials widened to such an extent in Midlands engineering and aircraft factories that there was official concern at the level of wages being paid.

While labor improved its position, it is generally suggested that women also improved their position within society and economically, with the exception of Nazi Germany where ideology consigned them to a more limited and specialized role. However, while women entered industry and the armed forces in increasing numbers it was not necessarily on a permanent basis. There was something of a revival of what might be termed female domesticity in postwar Britain, although there was a more permanent increase in the number of married and older women in employment. The war offered women opportunities for a wider freedom although this was very much a matter for individual perception.

Equally a matter of perception is how far social change occurred as a result of the war. There were certainly measurable trends: more marriages, more divorces, more illegitimate births, more crime – especially juvenile delinquency, usually attributed to the absence of fathers. In

Britain it can be shown statistically that more people attended cinemas and that more paid income tax than ever before. But there are also trends that cannot be measured. In Britain, for example, many commentators called the war a 'People's War,' and this was even a wartime propaganda slogan. There is the image of the happy communion of the London Underground stations during the Blitz, the 'Dunkirk Spirit' and so on. But it is clear from closer investigation that class differences persisted. Much was made of the evacuation of working-class women and children from the cities in 1939. In fact, it would seem that most of the hosts were also working-class rather than middle-class and the experience merely reinforced existing prewar analyses among middle-class observers. In any case, most had returned home before the bombing began. The war may have had temporary equalizing effects and thrown people of different classes together but it had little long-term impact on class differences or the ownership of property. Clearly, it would be hazardous to deny altogether the impact of evacuation, or for that matter the presence in Britain of over 1.5 million foreign servicemen; the British disinclination to differentiate between their treatment of white and colored American servicemen in this period produced particular tensions in the US services where segregation was practised – but it should not be overstated.

Few states went to war to transform society and yet the war did produce the ideals if not the reality of postwar social change and guided reconstruction. During the war in Britain an apparent consensus on guided change brought an education act, town and country planning act, Keynesian declarations of postwar full employment, and the establishment of a welfare state along the lines of the Beveridge Report of December 1942. Canada had its Marsh Report in 1943 and in the United States there were measures from which blacks and ex-servicemen theoretically benefited although, in the case of American blacks, discrimination continued irrespective of presidential directives to the contrary. In Britain the war did have a perceptible effect in a drift toward the political left reflected in the victory of the Labour Party in the 1945 election, but equally, the trend in the United States was to the political right.

Wartime changes may not have meant much in practical terms afterwards, although there was greater potential for change where a state collapsed or suffered total defeat. Change must also be seen in terms of long-term social trends over the course of a far longer period. Total war could not fail to generate some change but it is important to judge how far changes survived the immediate postwar period and how far such changes might have occurred in any case.

ABOVE: British women workers producing parts for Spitfires in early 1941.

ABOVE, FAR LEFT: Soviet partisans in northwest Russia – always a thorn in the side of the occupying forces.

FAR LEFT: Russian civilians view the results of German retaliation policies.

The Final Solution

The antipathy of the Nazis for the Jews was obvious long before Hitler came to power and the first of over 400 anti-Jewish laws was promulgated on 7 April 1933 within months of Hitler becoming German Chancellor. However, it was the conquest of Poland in September 1939 with a population of over two million Jews which appears to have made a 'final solution' to what the Nazis regarded as the Jewish 'problem' more attractive. In advance of the invasion of Russia, Hitler authorized Himmler, the head of the SS, to expand the *Einsatzgruppen* ('special action teams') which had been used to a limited extent in Poland. The teams would follow the German Army into Russia and eliminate communist commissars, others showing any degree of resistance to the Germans, and Jews. In that same summer – possibly as early as May and no later than July – both Himmler and Goering received Hitler's order to proceed with the extermination of the Jews. Goering tasked Heydrich, who headed the SS Security Service (SD), with carrying out the Führer's directive but, in effect, operational responsibility was that of Himmler.

Gas had already been used to exterminate the physically and mentally 'degenerate' in the Nazis' euthanasia program but the first death camp – which used mobile gas vans – did not open at Chelmno in Poland until December 1941. Belzec near Lublin opened in February 1942 and three more death camps in Poland – Sobidor, Majdanek and Treblinka – followed. The sixth camp – that at Auschwitz/Bergenau in Silesia – was converted from an ordinary concentration camp in March 1942. While earlier camps had experimented with carbon monoxide, Auschwitz's chambers were equipped with Zyklon B cyanide gas and proved grimly efficient.

The Jews of Europe fought back in at least 17 ghetto uprisings, the most significant of which was that at Warsaw in 1943, and there were at least nine areas of Poland or the Soviet Union in which Jewish partisans operated. There was, too, a revolt at Sobidor in which 400 prisoners escaped although the majority did not survive the attempt for long. Nevertheless, the Jewish population of occupied Europe as a whole was doomed, an estimated 5.9 million or 67 percent of the prewar Jewish population being annihilated by one means or another. In Poland, the Baltic States and Germany and Austria, over 90 percent of the prewar Jewish population failed to survive. Other groups such as the Slavs also suffered in the death camps although the process of extermination was somewhat slowed by the German need to use slave labor.

ABOVE: Jewish women and children under guard in the Warsaw ghetto in 1943. Many were later to die in extermination camps.

LEFT: Jews being transported to a concentration camp.

ABOVE RIGHT: Belsen after its liberation in April 1945.

RIGHT: Part of the women's barracks at Belsen. Deliberate overcrowding, poor food and the brutality of the camp guards led to the death of many inmates.

CHAPTER EIGHT

ONSLAUGHT IN THE EAST

The Soviet counterattack around Moscow in October 1941 forced the abandonment of the German offensive toward the capital on 8 December. Using the new T-34 tank, their truck-mounted Katyusha rockets and infiltration tactics, the Soviets threw the Wehrmacht back on the defensive along all fronts. General Meretskov's Fourth Army pushed von Leeb's Army Group North out of Tikhvin while von Rundstedt's Army Group South was compelled to quit the exposed salient toward Rostov by three Soviet armies attacking from the north. The recapture of Tikhvin in particular gave the Soviets improved access to Lake Ladoga over which they were now able to supply Leningrad during the winter months by running trucks over the ice. Later a railway was laid directly over the frozen surface but, still, possibly a million inhabitants died during the months of the siege.

Building on the success of his armies, Stalin ordered a general counteroffensive with the Soviet reserves. Hitler's refusal to allow retirements put the German armies in some peril but Zhukov's West Front Armies and the Kalinin Front Armies of General Konev exhausted themselves in trying to surround the German Fourth Panzer Army (formerly the 4th Panzer Group) and the Ninth Army around Vyazma in January 1942. Soviet parachute forces were dropped near to Vyazma but these and other Soviet troops were encircled in turn and eliminated by the Germans in March. A similar fate befell the Soviet Second Shock Army in the north three months later after Meretskov's Volkhov Front Armies had attempted to cut off the German Eighteenth Army. In the south, von Manstein also threw back the Soviet offensive but German battle casualties between November 1941 and March 1942 totaled 370,000: those from the harsh winter weather exceeded 500,000.

In the spring of 1942, Hitler resolved to continue the campaign. While the strategy adopted in 1941 had veered between an 'annihilation' strategy and an 'exhaustion' strategy, that in 1942 was purely 'exhaustion' and aimed at the rich economic resources of the Ukraine and the oilfields of the Caucasus. The idea had first been mooted by Hitler in July 1940 but detailed planning had only begun in the fall of 1941. Hitler's Directive No 41 of 5 April 1942 therefore gave priority to an advance toward the Caucasus with the seizure of Leningrad as a secondary objective. Now commanded by von Bock, Army Group South

PREVIOUS PAGES: Soviet troops in winter clothing on the attack in an attempt to relieve Leningrad.

ABOVE: German panzergrenadiers occupy a shallow foxhole during a lull in the fighting.

RIGHT: German troops from the Sixth Army in Stalingrad prepare to attack a Russian strongpoint.

LEFT: Soviet troops on the Leningrad front in 1942 occupy trenches in the lee of a knocked out Tiger tank.

was to seize the Crimea prior to eliminating Soviet forces around Iyzum on the Donets and driving south over the Don. To cover the flank of the thrust southward, three subsidary operations would be launched along the Don: an envelopment around Voronezh, an advance eastward from Kharkov, and a further push toward the city of Stalingrad on the Volga.

Although hampered by shortages in tanks, vehicles, and fuel, Army Group South beat off a Soviet spoiling attack around Iyzum between 12 and 18 May and quickly surrounded 214,000 Soviet troops in the Iyzum pocket. Von Manstein's Eleventh Army enjoyed equal success in taking 170,000 prisoners in the Crimea and Sebastopol fell to the Germans on 1 July. Hitler elevated von Manstein to Field Marshal and foolishly tasked Eleventh Army with the capture of Leningrad far to the north; four of the army's divisions were transferred at once. On 28 June 1942 the main push commenced with Hoth's Fourth Panzer Army and Second Army undertaking the first operation (Blue I) around Voronezh and General von Paulus' Sixth Army breaking through opposite Kharkov (Blue II). The First Panzer Army began its advance along the Don toward Stalingrad (Blue III) on 9 July. At this point, Hitler reorganized Army Group South. Von Bock, who had delayed sending Hoth south from Voronezh in view of signs of a Soviet build-up to the north of the city, was replaced altogether. General von Weichs was given command of Army Group B – principally Sixth Army and Hungarian, Rumanian and Italian troops – and Field Marshal List was given Army Group A controlling First and Fourth Panzer Armies and Seventeenth Army. In reality, Hitler had become *de facto* commander, especially of Army Group A, and interferred constantly in the succeeding military operations.

As a result of the changes, Hoth and von Kleist commanding First Panzer Army were delayed by being ordered to turn back to attempt an envelopment around Rostov which netted only 14,000 prisoners. This prevented von Paulus from pushing on to Stalingrad until Hoth could rejoin him later in July. On 23 July Hitler ordered Army Group A to push on into the Caucasus and as far down the Caspian Sea coast as Baku while Army Group B took Stalingrad and also pushed toward the Caspian. Inevitably, a gap began to develop. List's armies reached the Maikop oilfields on 9 August but could not do

so before the Soviets had set them alight and he then ran out of fuel short of the main Caucasian oilfields. When List reported on 6 September that he could go no farther, he was dismissed and Hitler himself assumed personal control of Army Group A. By now Hoth had been reassigned to Army Group B and was advancing on Stalingrad from the south, the city having become a major objective in itself. Hoth was halted by Soviet pressure but von Paulus reached the Volga river to the north of Stalingrad in late August.

Reorganized Soviet defenses around the city were placed under the control of General Chuikov's Sixty-second Army on 10 September. The Soviet defenders were soon pushed back into the city but the rubble produced by German air attack proved highly useful as an additional

BELOW: General Chuikov, the defender of Stalingrad.

BOTTOM: Soviet troops hold a settlement in the northern Caucasus region.

obstacle to the advancing Germans. Bitter and sustained house-to-house fighting ensued. However, von Paulus' army was now at the end of an exposed salient, the flanks of which were held only by Rumanians, Hungarians, and Italians. Halder gave up the unequal struggle to impose some reality on Hitler and accepted dismissal and retirement as Chief of Staff on 24 September. His replacement was General Zeitzler who had the reputation of being both optimistic and obedient. Hitler reiterated the suicidal standfast orders of December 1941 on 14 October 1942 by ordering all units to retain their positions until the spring.

RIGHT: Von Paulus surrendering at Stalingrad.

FAR LEFT: A Soviet 57mm anti-tank gun in action at Stalingrad.

CENTER, FAR LEFT: A German 37mm anti-tank crew in the stark ruins of Stalingrad.

LEFT: Some of Chuikov's troops of the Soviet Sixty-second Army at Stalingrad.

BELOW LEFT: Soviet troops crossing a river during the operations to surround the German Sixth Army.

BELOW: Some of the thousands of German prisoners taken at Stalingrad.

However, on 19 November the Soviets launched a major counterattack for which they had been planning since September: Operation Uranus. The Soviet Fifth Tank Army smashed through the Rumanians to the north of Stalingrad and, on the following day, the Fifty-first and Fifty-seventh Armies served out the same treatment to Rumanians in the south. The Soviet pincers closed on 23 November to encircle von Paulus' Sixth Army, IV Panzer Corps of Fourth Panzer Army, and two Rumanian divisions. Since Goering maintained that the Luftwaffe could keep the Stalingrad pocket supplied, Hitler refused von Paulus' request to break out. He also declined to withdraw Army Group A from the Caucasus to relieve Stalingrad and von Manstein was summoned from Leningrad to command a hastily organized Army Group Don which in reality amounted to little more than two divisions. The attempted relief, which began on 12 December, was halted after four days by a fresh Soviet offensive by Fifty-first Army while the Soviet First Guards and Sixth Armies also overran the Italians on the Don.

In Stalingrad itself the beleaguered Germans were progressively weakened by cold, hunger, and disease. The Luftwaffe would have needed to land 600 tons of supplies daily but could never manage more than 100 tons in face of freezing conditions, poor visibility, and anti-aircraft fire. Over 550 aircraft were lost from weather, accident, or hostile fire. On 19 December Hitler again refused to allow von Paulus to attempt a break out and his commander's request to begin negotiations on 22 January 1943. To encourage von Paulus, Hitler promoted him Field Marshal on 31 January but that same day von Paulus was captured as the last vestiges of resistance ceased. In fact, von Paulus stuck to the letter of Hitler's orders by only surrendering himself and his headquarters staff, other subordinate commands making their own surrender arrangements. An army of 230,000 had ceased to exist with 91,000 passing into captivity. Only 6000 would ever return to Germany.

LEFT: *Russian civilians shot in the prison yard at Rostov by retreating German troops in February 1943.*

CENTER LEFT: *A well-armed Soviet patrol on Leningrad's Pulkovo heights in 1943.*

RIGHT: *Soviet forces advance in the Kursk salient in 1943.*

FAR RIGHT: *A German Panther tank knocked out on the Eastern Front.*

RIGHT: *Soviet anti-tank crews and anti-tank riflemen during the Battle of Kursk. Note the abandoned German assault gun.*

BELOW: *Soldiers of the Red Army's Leningrad and Volkhov Fronts meet to lift the siege of Leningrad in 1943.*

A similar fate almost befell Army Group A in the Caucasus but Hitler was persuaded to allow a withdrawal from Rostov, which the Soviets recaptured on 14 February 1943. Kharkov was retaken on 16 February and von Manstein's Army Group Don, now renamed Army Group South, also faced encirclement. Von Manstein, however, gained Hitler's authority to reorganize by drawing additional units from Army Group A and concentrating armor for a counterblow. Von Manstein saw little point in a direct attack to retake Kharkov as Hitler was demanding and he also stood out against the temptation to use his scanty reserves for a defense of the Dniepr line. He wanted the Soviets to push on deeper despite the peril posed to the Germans so that he could launch a dislocating indirect blow against the hinge of the Soviet advance. On 19 February Hoth's reconstituted Fourth Panzer Army opened the offensive by striking northward into the salient formed by the Soviet advance. Kharkov once more fell to the Germans in mid-March and the Soviets were driven right back to the Donets. A 350-mile gap in the German front had been sealed after four months and the greatest Soviet winter offensive of the war was blunted despite Soviet superiority of eight to one in divisions. The Soviets had fought well in defense but could not endure the sudden change from triumphant advance to rapid withdrawal. It suggested that a defensive-offensive form of strategy was the key to paralyzing the Soviet menace. Elsewhere, Hitler also allowed retirement from exposed salients around Demyansk and Rzhev which made the German front shorter and easier to hold. The Soviets had finally broken the siege of Leningrad in the north on 12 January but Army Group North remained largely in place before the city.

Despite the failures of 1942 Hitler now wanted to seize the initiative and damage the offensive capability of the Red Armies. Von Manstein had rightly drawn the lesson that the best way forward was mobile defense to soak up Soviet attacks before launching armored counterattacks but Hitler, Zeitzler, and Field Marshal von Kluge (now commanding Army Group Center) favored outright offensive. On 15 April Hitler decided on Operation Citadel aimed at the Soviet salient around Kursk left after von Manstein's counterattack. From von Kluge's command, General Model's Ninth Army would attack from the north with six Panzer divisions while, from von Manstein's command, Hoth's Fourth Panzer Army and Group Kempf would attack from the south. The Germans would deploy some 1900 tanks in the double envelopment as well as 1700 airplanes and 1000 assault guns. However, not only was the operation postponed by bad weather but the Soviets were also well prepared and had constructed

Kursk

Kursk remains the greatest tank battle in history, the Germans massing 50 divisions including 16 Panzer divisions or motorized divisions amounting to 900,000 men with 10,000 guns, 2700 tanks or assault guns and over 2000 aircraft. The Soviets had also concentrated materiel along the likely axes of any German advance so that over the 345-mile front along which the battle was to rage they had an overall superiority of 1.4:1 in men, 2:1 in artillery, 1.3:1 in tanks and 1.2:1 in aircraft. In the sector held by the Soviet Thirteenth Army, for example, the Russians had 155 guns or heavy mortars per mile of front. Within their echeloned defense in depth, individual strongpoints might contain three to five artillery pieces, five anti-tank rifles and up to five mortars. In all, the Soviets mustered 1.3 million men, 20,000 guns, 3600 tanks and assault guns and 2400 aircraft.

Beginning their Operation Citadel on 5 July 1943, the German Fourth Panzer Army lost 200 tanks and over 25,000 casualties in pushing just six miles into the Soviet defenses of the Orel/Kursk salient in the first two days. While the Germans had to force their way through line after line of anti-tank defenses, the Soviets were able to push ever more reserves into the salient so that Fourth Panzer Army was brought to a virtual standstill after ten days.

The fiercest fighting occurred on 12 July around Prokhorovka and involved over 1500 German and Soviet tanks fighting at point-blank range. The two principal actions on this day saw II SS Panzer Corps ranged against Fifth Guards Tank Army and, in a subsidary role, XLVIII Panzer Corps ranged against First Tank Army supported by Sixth Guards Infantry Army. Three days later the Soviets opened their own counteroffensive which went on for 37 days and pushed the Germans back beyond Kharkov.

Precise figures for the losses on each side are uncertain since both Germans and Russians claimed to have knocked out more tanks than the other had. However, it seems likely that the two sides both lost about 50 percent of their armor.

Anti-tank Defenses

The lessons of Blitzkrieg in 1940 and 1941 appeared to be that the tank was now dominant on the battlefield, but by 1942 infantry and artillery were beginning to reassert themselves. Heavier towed anti-tank guns were introduced into the infantry line while the infantry also found an answer to armor in dispersion, depth of defense and their own portable hand-held antitank weapons such as the British PIAT, the American 6-cm rocket launcher or Bazooka and the German *Panzerfaust* recoilless weapon. The Germans also discovered that their 88mm anti-aircraft gun was highly effective in an anti-tank role.

A good example of how armor could be blunted came at Kursk between July and August 1943 where the Soviet defenses had an average depth of between 95 and 110 miles and in places, 180 miles. The Soviets had dug over 3100 miles of trenches and laid over 400,000 mines with an average density of 2400 antitank and 2700 antipersonnel mines per mile. On a rather more limited scale, the British armored offensive around Caen in July 1944 – Operation Goodwood – was halted by a defense of just ten miles in depth although tanks, self-propelled guns, six-barreled *Nebelwerfer* heavy mortars and antitank guns were carefully integrated around village strongpoints. Despite Allied aircraft dropping 5650 tons of bombs and artillery firing a one-and-a-half hour bombardment at the German positions, three British armored divisions were held by an understrength 21st Panzer Division and a field division.

defenses in depth and mustered 3300 tanks and over 20,000 guns. The bad weather persisted when the German attack opened on 4 July, and the Luftwaffe was unable to gain air superiority over the vast battlefield. Kursk became a brutal slogging match – the 'Death Ride of the Panzers' – and the largest tank battle of the war. With Soviet counterattacks against the Germans' Orel salient developing and the Allied invasion of Sicily, Hitler ordered the offensive stopped on 13 July. The II SS Panzer Corps was ordered to Italy and the Orel salient abandoned on 25 July to release still more troops for Italy and the Balkans. Withdrawal began on 22 August with Kharkov yet again being retaken by the Soviets on the following day. The Germans had lost over 500,000 men and half their total force of armor.

With the blunting of the Kursk offensive, the initiative once more passed to the Soviets who commenced their own attack against von Manstein's Army Group South on 17 July in the hope of trapping the Germans on the Dniepr and the Donets and pushing them out of the Ukraine. Using local superiority the Soviets launched a series of assaults over a broad front, forcing Hitler to recall troops from Italy and to order construction of defensive positions – the Panther and Wotan Lines. On 8 September Hitler allowed von Manstein to pull back to the Wotan Line but he would not make OKH solely responsible for the war against Russia as von Manstein and von Kluge urged. Army Group A was also permitted to quit the Kuban for the relative safety of the Crimea.

Unfortunately, the retirement of the reconstituted Sixth Army led to Seventeenth Army being isolated in the Crimea. In many cases, too, the Soviets reached the Dniepr before the Germans could while the Wotan Line existed only in name. Kiev fell into Soviet hands again on 3 November, although the attempt to push beyond Kiev was halted by the return of troops recalled from Italy. In the north the Soviets also made progress along the boundary between Army Group North and Army Group Center, the latter being pushed out of Smolensk. Much of the Panther position was lost by late November. The Soviet offensive continued with further operations against Army Group South in December which succeeded in surrounding the German XL and XLII Corps around Korsun but they were able to fight their way out. Army Group North also faced further attacks in January 1944 which pushed the Germans back from Leningrad. Hitler allowed Model, who now commanded in the north, to retire to the remains of the Panther position along the frontiers of Estonia and Latvia on 15 February 1944.

Desperately short of men and materiel, the Germans

were again forced back in the Ukraine in March. Hitler wanted various locations turned into fortresses and held to the last man, but von Manstein was able to save First Panzer Army from being caught in a trap on the Dniepr by flying personally to Hitler's Berchtesgaden retreat to convince the Führer that they must be allowed to break out. His reward was to be dismissed along with von Kluge on 30 March. Model replaced von Manstein and General Schoerner replaced von Kluge. By early April, however, while First Panzer Army had effected its escape, the Germans had lost the Ukraine. In the Crimea, Seventeenth Army was attacked in April and over 30,000 men left in Soviet hands as the Germans hastily evacuated the port of Sebastopol.

Three leading Soviet marshals – Zhukov, Rokossovsky and Vasilevsky – now fell on Army Group Center with the aim of breaking through the German front to close on Minsk. Operation Bagration began on 22 June and in under two weeks destroyed the German Fourth and Ninth Armies. Army Group Center, command of which was given to Model in addition to his duties farther south, had little armor, and the Allied invasion of Normandy further

ABOVE RIGHT: Soviet seamen advance against the retreating Germans during the recapture of Sebastopol in April 1944.

TOP LEFT: A medium artillery battery of the 4th Ukrainian Group in the Carpathians during 1944.

LEFT: A column of German prisoners near Karsun-Shevchenkovsky on the Second Ukrainian Front.

RIGHT: Troops of the Red Army's First Byelorussian Front move through a German-occupied wood near Bobruisk.

LEFT: A Soviet 45mm anti-tank gun on the outskirts of Sebastopol in April 1944.

RIGHT: A smashed German 105mm battery near Minsk in December 1944.

reduced the scope for moving troops as reinforcements to Russia. Minsk itself fell on 4 July and it was not until August that any semblance of stability was achieved in the German lines. By this time, however, Army Group North, now commanded by Schoerner, was all but cut off in the Baltic states. The Soviets were also over the Vistula and within striking distance of Warsaw.

The Polish resistance – the Polish Home Army – chose this moment to stage an insurrection in the city. The Poles had always contemplated doing so to coincide with the arrival of Allied forces, Operation Burza being envisaged as a series of rolling revolts region by region as the Soviets advanced into Poland. The failure of earlier risings, including that of Warsaw's Jewish ghetto in April 1943, did not deter the Home Army leadership and on 1 August 1944 fighting broke out across the city. The Poles appealed for assistance which the western Allies tried to supply by air dropping materiel to the west of Warsaw. However, the pleas of Churchill and Roosevelt to Stalin to be allowed to use Soviet airfields were ignored in Moscow until 9 September, and the Soviets proved unable or unwilling to cross the Vistula in sufficient force to aid the Poles directly. By 2 October the Home Army had been destroyed. Some 200,000 Poles died in the fighting while the Germans suffered 26,000 casualties. A lingering suspicion was that Stalin had deliberately sacrificed the Poles – he had referred to the Home Army as a 'group of criminals' – especially when the Soviets had also murdered over 14,000 Polish officers they had captured in 1939. The bodies of 4300 of these victims had been discovered by the Germans at Katyn in April 1943.

In the north, the Finns had also been forced back by the Soviet offensive and they concluded a peace agreement with the Soviet Union on 2 September 1944. Farther south, Soviet troops crossed into Rumania and Bulgaria, and the German Sixth Army again suffered total annihilation on the Prut river in August 1944. On 25 August Rumania declared war on Germany, King Carol had had Antonescu arrested and agreed to an armistice with the Soviets two days previously. The Soviets formally declared war on

Soviet Partisans

The nucleus of the early Soviet partisan bands were Red Army soldiers cut off by the speed of the German advance although other Russians took up arms after a public broadcast by Stalin on 3 July 1941 urging guerrilla resistance. Great stress was always placed on strict party control of the partisans, and a Central Staff of the Partisan Movement was established in Moscow under the command of Lieutenant General Ponomarenko. Operations were also planned in close co-operation with the main Soviet armies, the Soviet interpretation of partisan warfare being the traditional one of irregulars operating in the rear or on the flanks of an enemy in support of conventional military operations.

However, the Germans generally enjoyed success against the Soviet partisans to such an extent that the 400,000 or 500,000 partisans that existed by the end of 1943 may well have represented something of a waste of Soviet resources. The Germans did not garrison large parts of the Russian countryside and German commanders were not necessarily concerned by partisan activity in their rear. The Soviet partisans did become of account after Hitler had begun to insist on last-ditch resistance and no retirements, but by that time the partisans were increasingly being absorbed back into the main Red armies. The Germans did not produce the standard manual *Warfare Against Bands* until the autumn of 1944, and tended to leave the task of internal security largely to the second-rate Italian, Rumanian, and Hungarian units and other formations raised from Russian minorities willing to co-operate against the Soviets.

Bulgaria on 5 September and within three days the Bulgarians had also capitulated and declared war on Germany in turn. In Hungary Horthy also appeared poised to change sides but in Operation *Panzerfaust* Otto Skorzeny, who had been responsible for Mussolini's rescue from detention, spearheaded a German coup against the Hungarian government on 15 October. This kept Hungary in the war, and Budapest continued to be held at Hitler's insistence until its garrison was overwhelmed on 11 February 1945. Even then Hitler tried to mount a counterattack but it failed; the Soviets drove into Austria on 28 March and Vienna fell on 13 April.

By this time Soviet forces were also well into Czechoslovakia. In August 1944 when the Soviets were approaching Slovakia, the Germans had flooded in troops to safeguard their rear. These troops clashed with the Slovaks but this 'Slovak Rising' was easily contained and the partisans were forced up into the Tatra mountains. It had not been until October and November 1944 that the Soviets were able to cross the Carpathians into Slovakia. Progess thereafter had been slow and it was not until 11 May 1945 that the last German in Czechoslovakia capitulated, six days after a rising in Prague in which the German-backed Vlasov Army joined the insurgents.

ABOVE LEFT: One of the feared Soviet Katyusha rocket batteries is prepared for action.

RIGHT: A German supply column after a Soviet artillery strike.

LEFT: The mass grave of Polish officers murdered at Katyn Wood, a picture taken after its discovery by the Germans.

RIGHT: A German King Tiger tank in Budapest during the summer of 1944.

The last major Soviet offensive against Germany was prepared by Zhukov, Konev, and Rokossovsky. Rokossovsky would advance to Danzig on the Baltic while Zhukov attempted an envelopment of Warsaw and Konev advanced on Breslau from the Vistula. The offensive began on 12 January 1945 after the western Allies had pressed for its commencement to help relieve the pressure of the German Ardennes offensive in Belgium. It was an immediate success and Warsaw fell to Zhukov on 17 January followed by Lodz three days later, while Konev and Rokossovsky also advanced satisfactorily. Zhukov therefore recommended that the offensive be continued and he secured a bridgehead on the Oder on 2 February. The only available German reserve – Sixth SS Panzer Army – was diverted to the abortive relief of Budapest and a half-hearted counterattack by Eleventh SS Panzer Army in Pomerania was soon halted. Danzig fell on 30 March and, fearing the Allies might attempt to get to Berlin first, Stalin directed Zhukov and Konev to go straight on for the German capital. The last Soviet push began on 16 April, Berlin being completely surrounded by the 25th.

On the same day Soviet troops came into contact with advanced elements of the US 69th Infantry Division on the Elbe. The Soviet First, Second, Third, and Eighth Guards Tank Armies, the Third and Fifth Shock Armies, and the Twenty-eighth Army drove into Berlin. By 28 April the German perimeter had been reduced to only ten miles by three miles. A final assault was now prepared to take the Soviets into Hitler's last refuge around the Reichstag.

ABOVE: One of the last photographs of Hitler, inspecting boy soldiers in Berlin during April 1945.

LEFT: German paratroopers prepare to stem the tide of the Soviet attack on the Eastern Front.

RIGHT: The first Soviet T-34 tanks enter the Berlin suburbs after fighting their way through the capital's outer defenses.

LEFT: Soviet infantry and armor clear Frauensburg of the enemy.

RIGHT: Hoisting the Red Flag over Berlin's Reichstag building.

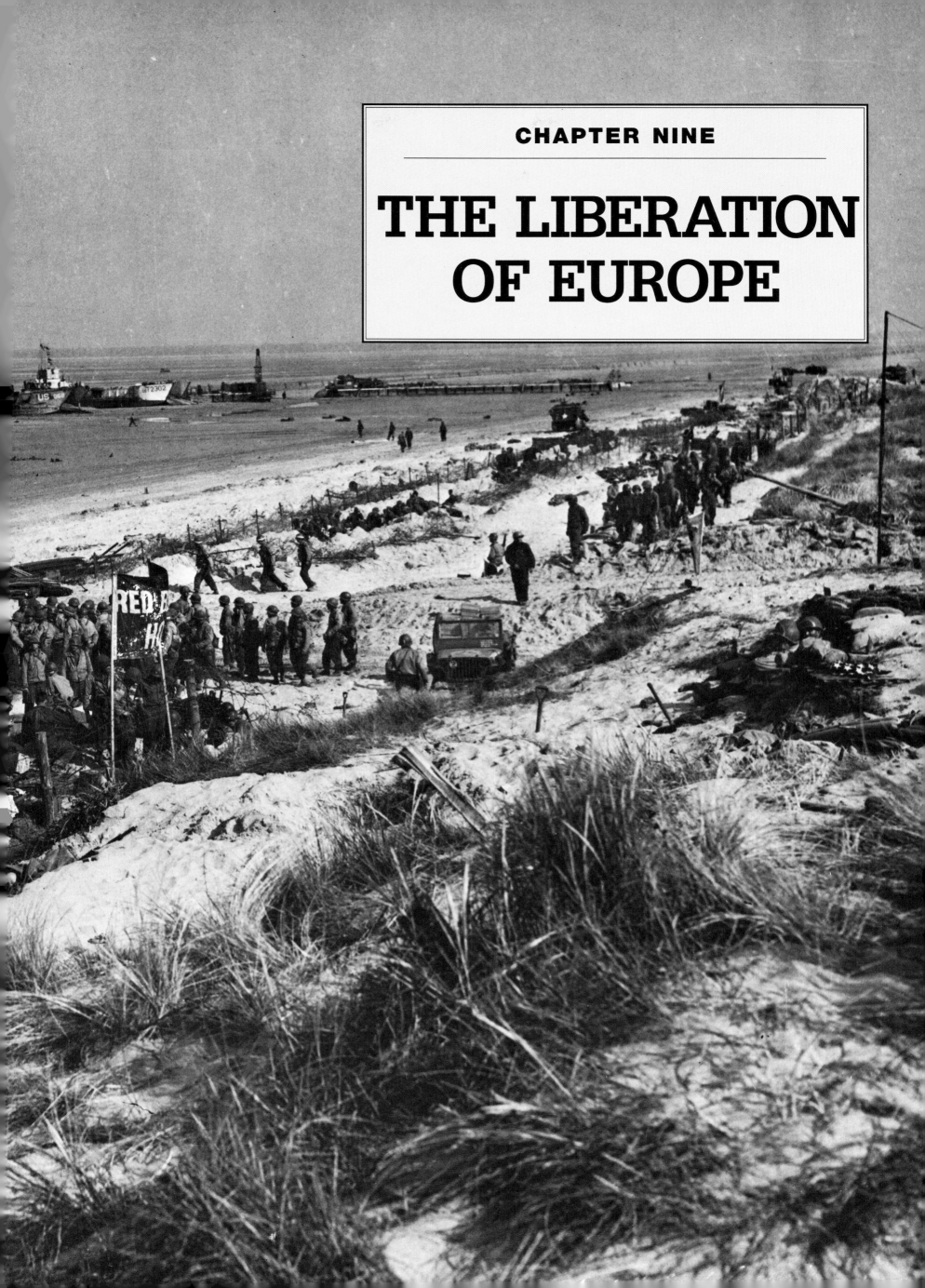

CHAPTER NINE

THE LIBERATION OF EUROPE

The fighting which encompassed the globe from December 1941 onward was in fact two separate but concurrent wars. One was fought primarily in Europe and immediately adjoining areas against Germany, Italy, and their allies, while the other was fought in Southeast Asia and the Pacific against Japan. Of the two wars, the European war was the more important because both the United States and Britain recognized that victory over Germany would ensure the defeat of Japan whereas the reverse was not the case. Nevertheless, the war in Europe would remain a series of almost unrelated campaigns in the Mediterranean, Russia, at sea and in the air until the Allies could mount a 'second front' against Germany. This is not to dismiss the campaign in Italy after September 1943, but in strategic terms the roads north from Rome led nowhere. A second front in northwestern Europe would be a genuine threat to German survival.

As early as the summer of 1940 Churchill ordered preparations to begin for fighting the way back on to the continent. Indeed, the first commandos were established on 5 June 1940 and raids were mounted against Le Touquet in late June and against the German-held Channel Islands in July, the same month in which Admiral of the Fleet Sir Roger Keyes was appointed Director of Combined Operations. In March 1941 commandos staged a more ambitious raid on the Lofoten Islands off Norway and, in early tentative discussions with the Americans – known as the ABC-1 talks – Churchill secured their adherence to the idea of an eventual cross-Channel invasion to defeat Germany should they enter the war at a later stage. Thus, when the Americans did come into the war in December 1941, the Arcadia Conference in Washington swiftly adopted the concept of 'Germany First.' In fact, the United States planners were to push for the cross-Channel invasion rather more forcibly than the British who came to prefer exploiting the opportunities that appeared to exist in the Mediterranean.

At Arcadia the invasion was penciled in for 1944 but in early 1942 the Americans proposed a build up (code-named 'Bolero') in Britain leading to an invasion with 48 divisions ('Roundup') in 1943 or conceivably even an emergency effort ('Sledgehammer') in 1942 if Russia faced collapse. The British did not like the Sledgehammer option and successfully vetoed it, but they were also skeptical of Roundup and argued for Mediterranean operations instead at the Casablanca Conference in January 1943. At the Washington Trident Conference in May 1943 it was finally decided to attempt an invasion by 1 May 1944 with 29 divisions, seven of which would have to be withdrawn from the Mediterranean no later than November 1943. The new invasion plan ('Roundhammer') was approved by the Joint Chiefs of Staff on 9 August and endorsed by the Quebec Conference although Churchill personally was still wedded to the Mediterranean and also suggested a possible operation against Norway ('Jupiter'). At the Cairo and Tehran Conferences the projected date slipped back to 31 May 1944 due to the shortages of landing craft and continuing operations in Italy.

Despite the disagreements between the Allies, the detailed planning for the cross-Channel invasion had continued. In June 1942 the then Brigadier General Eisenhower had been dispatched to London as Commanding General of the US Army European Theater of Operations (ETOUSA) in order to co-ordinate planning with the British. Eisenhower continued as ETOUSA as well as Supreme Commander in North Africa until February 1943 but was then subsequently appointed Supreme Commander for the invasion – now renamed 'Overlord' – in December. In April of that year, detailed planning had been entrusted to a separate joint staff headed by the British Lieutenant General Frederick Morgan as Chief of Staff to the Supreme Allied Commander (COSSAC). In turn, COSSAC drew on earlier work by the so-called Com-

bined Commanders, representing the three British armed services, ETOUSA and Commodore Lord Louis Mountbatten, who had succeeded Keyes as Director of Combined Operations in October 1941.

The earlier planning had already identified Normandy as a more favorable area than the Pas de Calais for landings because the latter was too well defended. Normandy could provide large beaches; better climatic conditions in terms of tide, wind, and sea approaches; and provided Cherbourg could be seized at an early stage there would be adequate port facilities. It was also within fighter range from southern England and would be more difficult for the Germans to reinforce rapidly. Consequently, Morgan's staff confirmed the choice of Normandy in June 1943 and elaborate deception plans were put in hand to persuade the Germans that either Norway or the Pas de Calais were the real objectives.

There were no illusions as to the difficulty of mounting an invasion, especially after Mountbatten's 'reconnaissance in force' (Operation Jubilee) against Dieppe on 19 August 1942. This followed further commando raids on Vaagso in Norway in December 1941 and the Normandie dock at St Nazaire in March 1942. The first British parachute assault had also been in the nature of a raid on a German radio station at Bruneval in France in February. It had been thought that Dieppe was only garrisoned lightly when in fact the Germans had over 5000 men in the vicinity and others in reserve. While British commandos were reasonably successful in securing their objectives, Major-General Roberts' 2nd Canadian Division suffered heavy casualties landing across open shingle beaches over which supporting tanks could not pass easily. Royal Navy gunfire proved inadequate and 34 vessels were lost including the destroyer HMS *Berkeley*. The RAF also lost heavily, 106 aircraft going down in major air battles over the town. In all there were 3670 casualties in the landing troops and 29 tanks were abandoned on the beaches. By contrast, the Germans had lost just 591 casualties and Hitler ordered more rapid construction of his 'Atlantic Wall,' work on which had begun in March.

At the same time, Field Marshal von Rundstedt had been appointed Commander in Chief in the West. In November 1943 Rommel, who had been commanding Army Group B in Italy, was directed to inspect the west European coast and report direct to OKW. In January 1944 he became commander of a new Army Group B in France comprising Fifteenth and Seventeenth Armies with responsibility for defeating any invasion. But Rommel's appointment still left von Rundstedt in overall command. This was to cause some difficulties since both wanted to control German reserves. A compromise gave Rommel three panzer divisions but four others including a panzer grenadier division were attached to OKW reserve which von Rundstedt erroneously assumed that he would control in the battle.

Morgan's original scheme had envisaged employing two British and one American division in the first assault with the object of establishing a bridgehead which could be expanded to include Cherbourg and Caen by D-Day +

Airborne Assault

The earliest pioneer of airborne assault was the Red Army whose dropping of 1200 paratroopers during their 1936 maneuvers astonished foreign military attachés. However, although making some use of airborne forces during the Russo-Finnish War, the Soviets did not utilize them to any great extent against the Germans. Nevertheless, the Red Army's early experimentation had some impact in Germany, where parachute units were first formed in 1935 by the Luftwaffe after observing Soviet forces under the provisions of the Rapallo Treaty. German airborne forces were then used to seize Vienna's Wagram airfield at the start of the *Anschluss* in March 1938 and airlanding of troops, which the Germans had practised during the Spanish Civil War,

was employed in the Sudetenland in October 1938. The first Luftwaffe parachute divisions appeared in 1939 and airborne assault proved successful in Norway, France, and the Low Countries in 1940. Ironically, while the battle for Crete in 1941 proved catastrophic for the German airborne forces and led to Hitler losing interest in the concept, it encouraged the British and Americans to press ahead with their own airborne experiments. However, the Allied experience on Sicily and in Normandy and especially during Operations Market Garden and Varsity (Arnhem and the Rhine crossing respectively) was not a happy one. Indeed, it might be argued that airborne forces were simply not cost-effective in terms of the resources devoted to them.

US paratroopers en route for Normandy.

LEFT: *Anxious American troops going ashore on D-Day.*

TOP, FAR RIGHT: *Commandos of 155 Brigade approaching Sword Beach opposite Ouistreham.*

CENTER, FAR RIGHT: *The 3rd Canadian Division landing at Courselles on Juno Beach.*

BOTTOM RIGHT: *Men of the 13/18th Hussars loaded on to LCTs for the Channel crossing.*

BELOW: *US forces on Omaha Beach. Note the abandoned half-tracks and the infantry pinned down at the water's edge, while the landing craft bow-gunner engages targets with a 20mm cannon.*

14. A second US division was later added to secure the Cotentin peninsula, the American formations coming under US First Army commanded by Lieutenant General Omar Bradley and the British under Second Army commanded by Lieutenant General Sir Miles Dempsey. Both Bradley and Dempsey came within the orbat of Twenty-first Army Group to which Montgomery was appointed in December 1943. However, Montgomery wanted the invasion frontage increased to include a fifth division and airborne forces on the flanks. This was eventually accepted but it again required additional landing craft which could only be obtained by postponing D-Day until 1 June and delaying Operation Anvil in southern France. Other disagreements surrounded the strategic direction of Allied airpower in support of the landings, Eisenhower being given control of the Allied bombers from April until September 1944. This resulted in a sustained aerial attack on the German transportation system in France and on the Luftwaffe's airfields.

While D-Day was scheduled for 1 June, Eisenhower had some flexibility. Tide and moon would be right on 5, 6, or 7 June before the next favorable date of 19 June, and on 17 May Eisenhower opted for the 5th. Then bad weather postponed the operation for 24 hours, and Allied airborne troops finally dropped over Normandy in the first minutes of 6 June 1944. US 82nd and 101st Airborne Divisions were dropped behind Utah beach in order to secure the inland causeways for US VII Corps due to land there, while the British 6th Airborne Division was to hold the left flank of the beachhead west of Sword beach and Juno beach where British I Corps would land. Both British and American paratroopers became widely scattered but they were able to reach the majority of their objectives. In the case of 6th Airborne Division this included the Merville battery and the bridges over the Orne river and Caen canal. The Germans had been caught almost completely by surprise, Rommel having left the day before for Germany to join his wife for her birthday and to attempt to see Hitler to get more reserves released to his control. While not convinced that Normandy was more than a feint, von Rundstedt did decide to order up the 12th SS Panzer and Panzer Lehr Divisions at about 0330 on 6 June. But as these were OKW formations, Hitler's staff refused to authorize release unless the Führer consented and declined to wake him to ask.

By this time, the Allied armada was fast approaching the landing beaches, H-Hour being set at 0630 on the American beaches of Utah and Omaha (V Corps) and at 0730 for the British beaches of Gold (XXX Corps), Sword, and Juno. Only two German aircraft made any kind of attack on the beaches during the morning and German coastal batteries were generally ineffective. Landing went reasonably smoothly on the British beaches where troops were greatly assisted by the 'funnies' – a variety of specially adapted tanks for clearing minefields and other obstacles. At Utah the leading elements landed 2000 yards south of the intended beach by error but fortuitously in a less well-defended spot. Only on Omaha was there a major problem, the defenses being held by the determined German 352nd Infantry Division. A third of the day's casualties – 1000 – occurred on Omaha and convinced the Germans that they had defeated the invasion attempt. Although successfully ashore the Allies had not taken Caen which was a first day objective since the British advance had been held up by the only immediately available German reserves of 21st Panzer Division. Indeed, the beaches were not linked up until 10 June and not effectively secure until two days after that.

Nonetheless, the Germans had been unable to react decisively enough. Hitler did not wake until mid-morning and the OKW reserve panzer divisions were only released at 1530. The 12th SS Panzer Division did not reach Caen until 7 June and the Panzer Lehr, much hampered by

FAR LEFT: *American troops edging along the road to St Lo.*

LEFT: *No 3 Platoon of the 1st Dorsets firing their mortars at enemy positions in Hottot.*

RIGHT: *The ruins of Caen in July 1944.*

BOTTOM LEFT: *US soldiers look over a German anti-tank gun caught by an airstrike near Marigny.*

BELOW: *German troops defend the ruins of Caen.*

BOTTOM: *A Churchill tank of the British 79th Armored Division and Bren-gun carriers move through a village in Normandy.*

Allied bombing, only on the 9th. Counterattacks were attempted but the Allied build-up was faster than that of the Germans, over 326,000 men were ashore by 12 June with complete air superiority. Allied deception plans also continued to mislead Hitler who halted reserves en route to Normandy from northern France, information which was soon in Allied hands through ULTRA. Nor did the Germans take sufficient advantage from the severe storms between 17 and 22 June, which caused considerable damage to the artificial Mulberry harbors brought across the Channel in prefabricated sections to serve as a port until Cherbourg was captured. The storms made Cherbourg all the more important and US VII Corps, which began a drive across the Cotentin peninsula on 14 June, closed on the port by 21 June. Hitler ordered that it be held to the last man but Allied aircraft, ships, and artillery pounded the garrison into submission on the 26th. However, the Germans had done a thorough job of demolition and the port was not operable until August.

Despite the capture of Cherbourg and the failure of German counterattacks, the campaign was still to prove controversially protracted. The key was Caen to which most German reinforcements had gravitated. Montgomery was obliged to make virtue out of necessity and tackle the Germans at their strongest point on the direct route to Paris. Thus, the British and Canadians fought a series of actions of which the most significant were 'Epsom' (25 June-2 July), 'Charnwood' (4-10 July) and 'Goodwood' (18-20 July) to clear Caen. The latter was the last and most costly British armored offensive of the war. Despite massive carpet bombing, a tactic employed on several occasions during the Normandy campaign, the British lost 437 out of 877 tanks committed against German defenses in depth. They had lacked sufficient infantry and artillery support over ground ill suited to armored warfare. While it enabled the Canadians to take Caen on 19 July, 'Goodwood' did not prove the decisive breakthrough that Montgomery almost certainly intended. Its failure led him to claim that the real intention all along had been to hold the Germans at Caen and 'write down' their armor sufficiently to let the Americans break out in the west. But the Americans had little armor ashore and faced difficult bocage hedgerow terrain so that by the end of July the bridgehead showed little change from that of mid-June.

The July Plot

The origins of the July Plot lay in the loose conspiracy among German general staff officers prior to the war. In 1944 those most closely implicated were either retired officers or those serving in reserve headquarters such as the *Ersatzheer* and *Wehrkreise* in Berlin and in the headquarters of the military administrations in Brussels and Paris, although Army Group Center was also involved. A few civilians were in the conspiracy and also members of the German military intelligence service, the *Abwehr*. An earlier attempt to kill Hitler had failed in March 1943 when a bomb placed in his aircraft failed to detonate while other attempts at assassination were aborted for one reason or another. Finally, in July 1944, Lieutenant Colonel Count Claus von Stauffenberg volunteered to place a bomb in Hitler's Wolf's Lair headquarters at Rastenberg in East Prussia. Once Hitler was dead it was intended to activate army units with the codeword *Valkyrie* which had been dis-

guised as an operation to cordon off principal buildings in Berlin and elsewhere in the event of an uprising by foreign laborers. On 20 July von Stauffenberg placed his bomb in a briefcase against a table leg close to Hitler and made his escape from the building. The explosion, which occurred at 1242, convinced him that Hitler was dead when, in fact, another officer had moved the briefcase further away from the *Führer* quite fortuitously and Hitler emerged shaken but alive. Innumerable delays took place in putting the coup into effect and Hitler's survival sealed the fate of the conspiracy. Among those executed were von Stauffenberg, Field Marshal von Witzleben and Generals von Tresckow, von Stülpnagel and Hoepner. Other generals involved committed suicide including the former Chief of Staff, Beck, and von Kluge and Rommel. At the same time, Zeitzler was dismissed as Army Chief of Staff and replaced by Guderian.

Hitler and Mussolini view the damage after the bomb plot.

Army commanded by Lieutenant General Hodges – Bradley had been elevated to command 12th Army Group – holding at Mortain while Patton's Third Army drove north and the British and Canadians south. The moves might have caught the German 5th Panzer and Seventh Armies in the Mortain-Argentan-Falaise salient, but Bradley chose to halt Patton's formations at Argentan when the American advance threatened to go too far too fast, while Montgomery neglected to give the Canadians sufficient support. The Germans therefore managed to extract 20-40,000 men (they lost 50,000 as prisoners) before the Americans and Canadians linked up on 19 August. There was now no alternative for the Germans but to retreat and Field Marshal Model, who had replaced von Kluge, adhered to his predecessor's plans. On 15 August American and Free French forces had landed in southern France and were advancing rapidly up the Rhone valley.

Eisenhower had now decided to abandon the earlier intention of pausing on the Seine to build up supplies and he proposed to press ahead. The advance would still adhere to the original concept of a broad advance to carry Montgomery's 21st Army Group of First Canadian and Second British Armies to the Ruhr and Low Countries, and Bradley's 12th Army Group of Hodges' First and Patton's Third Armies toward the Saar. However, Montgomery preferred to place all resources behind a single narrow thrust to the Ruhr. Eisenhower was prepared to envisage Hodges being diverted to assist 21st Army Group and to give him priority over Patton in fuel but no more. It did not please Eisenhower's American subordinates but nor did it satisfy Montgomery who continued to advocate what became known as the 'narrow front' strategy as a quicker means of defeating Germany.

Paris, which Eisenhower had intended to bypass, rose in revolt against the Germans on 19 August. The situation was only saved by General von Choltitz's decision not to destroy the city as Hitler demanded and the city was surrendered on 25 August. By the first week of September the greater part of France was clear. Brussels fell to the British on 3 September and the great prize of the port of Antwerp was taken intact on the following day although it took until 28 November to clear German forces from the Scheldt waterway between Antwerp and the sea. By 12 September Patton had also linked with the forces advancing from southern France.

At this point the advance faltered through increasing logistic difficulties, the Americans in particular outstripping their supply lines. Montgomery was still insistent on a single thrust to carry him across the Rhine before the

Nevertheless, German strength was being eroded at rates faster than could be covered and Allied airpower was becoming an even more formidable weapon against German tanks. On 17 July Rommel himself was badly injured when his staff car was attacked by British aircraft near Livarot. Von Rundstedt had been retired by Hitler on 2 July and Field Marshal von Kluge now took over both overall command in the West and Rommel's Army Group B. Three days after Rommel's injury, Hitler survived an attempt on his life at his Wolf's Lair headquarters in East Prussia. The 'July Plot' was to have profound consequences not least for von Kluge who was implicated and, when relieved of his command on 19 August, he committed suicide. Rommel was also to fall victim to Hitler's wrath and took the 'honorable' death forced upon him on 14 October.

Even while the results of the 'July Plot' unfolded the Allied breakout had begun, Bradley's US First Army launching Operation Cobra on 25 July. By 31 July the Americans had broken clear of Avranches and moved initially into Brittany then eastward toward the Seine. Hitler ordered a counterattack toward Avranches on 6 August. Alerted by ULTRA, the Allies were well prepared, First

ABOVE: *Parisians scatter for cover as a German sniper opens fire on the Place de la Concorde, 26 August 1944.*

RIGHT: *King or Royal Tiger tanks of the German SS Leibstandarte Division in France, 1944.*

LEFT: *M4 Shermans advance through a French town.*

ABOVE: British paratroopers with a mortar at Arnhem in September 1944.

ABOVE, FAR RIGHT: German troops advance in Nijmegen.

ABOVE LEFT: The US 82nd Airborne Division dropping over Nijmegen.

LEFT: US airborne forces with the wreckage of one of their gliders at Nijmegen.

BOTTOM, FAR RIGHT: German defenders near the bridge at Arnhem.

Germans could organize an effective defense. On 10 September Eisenhower accepted part of the Montgomery plan – the idea of using Lieutenant General Brereton's 1st Allied Airborne Army to seize a bridgehead across the Rhine at Arnhem while British XXX Corps drove to Arnhem along an 'airborne carpet' secured across seven intervening bridges. Operation Market Garden envisaged that the US 101st Airborne Division would seize Eindhoven, the US 82nd Airborne Division six further bridges including Nijmegen, and British 1st Airborne division, later reinforced by 1st Polish Parachute Brigade, would take Arnhem. It was an enormous gamble which ignored evidence of the presence of both Model and 9th and 10th SS Panzer Divisions in the Arnhem area in the belief that the operation would unhinge the German reaction. It almost worked since the Americans took most of the necessary bridges on 17 September but the British landings were dispersed and hit by breakdowns in communications. In turn, XXX Corps could not maintain progress up the single road stretching almost 80 miles to Arnhem. It closed near to Arnhem on 22 September but could not effect a relief and the surviving British and Polish paratroopers broke out on the night of 25 September. Of nearly 10,000 men sent into Arnhem only 2163 escaped. A total of 1130 were killed and 6450 taken prisoner. The whole operation cost the Allies 11,850 casualties and, though it secured the Maas and Waal crossings, it was considerably less than had been hoped. It also gave the Germans valuable breathing space.

Montgomery was now directed by Eisenhower to give priority to the Schelde while a series of offensives along the length of the front gave the Allies local gains without real significance save Alsace-Lorraine which was largely cleared with the exception of a German salient around Colmar. The Allies had resigned themselves to a winter campaign of slow and unspectacular progress. Then, to their considerable surprise, the Germans launched a massive counterattack in the Ardennes on 16 December 1944. Hitler had managed to assemble two tank armies by ruthlessly stripping manpower and materiel from other fronts and by allocating virtually all new war production to equipping them. In the depth of winter these armies – General von Manteuffel's 5th Panzer Army and General Sepp Dietrich's 6th SS Panzer Army – were to drive for Antwerp through the weakest part of the Allied line where Hodges' US First Army held the Monschau-Echternach sector of the Ardennes. What might happen subsequently was not apparently considered and maintaining the momentum would depend upon capturing Allied stocks of fuel in the advance.

A special Panzer Brigade 150 was also assembled under command of Skorzeny to sow confusion by disguising themselves in American uniforms and to seize the Meuse bridges. Paratroopers would also be dropped at Monschau. In the event, neither paratroopers nor Skorzeny's men contributed much to the offensive – the parachute assault was postponed and Skorzeny failed to take the bridges. However, they did add to the chaos behind the American front and Operation *Wacht am Rhein* ('Watch on the Rhine') achieved total surprise. German care and security denied the Allies the usual ULTRA intelligence. The brunt of the attack fell on Major General Middleton's US VIII Corps and Major General Gerow's US V Corps. The latter was driven back on the Elsenborn ridge and the important road junction at St Vith fell into German hands on 21 December. However, its defense had slowed down the German advance. In the south, VIII Corps crumbled but 101st Airborne Division under the temporary command of Brigadier General Anthony McAuliffe was able to reinforce the equally important nodal center of Bastogne before it was encircled. It was McAuliffe who delivered the celebrated response of 'Nuts' to a demand to surrender on 22 December.

Meanwhile, Eisenhower had directed Montgomery from the north and Bradley from the south to pinch in the developing German salient. Together with determined American resistance, clearing skies which helped Allied aircraft to bring their full weight of firepower to bear, and dwindling German fuel supplies, Eisenhower's strategy ensured that the German effort was all but spent by Christmas Day. On 8 January 1945 Hitler authorized Model to break off the action. The opening of the Soviet offensive in the east four days later led to the withdrawal of Sixth SS Panzer Army eastward and by 28 January the Allied line had been fully restored. The Allies had lost over 76,000 casualties but the Germans had lost 70,000 with a further 50,000 captured and their last real reserves of manpower exhausted. One more limited German attack was mounted in Lorraine in January which briefly threatened Strasbourg but thereafter the initiative in the war lay wholly with the Allies.

ABOVE RIGHT: Young German soldiers guarded by members of the US 3rd Army at Magorette during the Ardennes offensive.

RIGHT: American prisoners during the early stages of the Ardennes attack.

ABOVE, FAR RIGHT: A German tank passes a column of Americans taken prisoner in the Ardennes.

FAR RIGHT: A tank destroyer of the US 703rd Tank Destroyer Battalion passing a disabled German tank south of Langlir in Belgium, 13 January 1945.

RIGHT: *Allied gliders in a field near Hemminkeln after the Rhine crossing on 25 March 1945.*

LEFT: *Troops of the US Seventh Army landing from their assault boat on the east bank of the Rhine near Frankenthal on 26 March 1945.*

BELOW LEFT: *Soldiers responsible for the taking of the bridge at Remagen record their stories for a US broadcast, 7 March 1945.*

With the Russians sweeping across the Oder, the western Allies also advanced. From 8 February onward, increased pressure was exerted on German forces remaining west of the Rhine, a series of clearing actions being fought. Montgomery still wanted his narrow thrust but the actions fought collectively indicated Eisenhower's broad front strategy. The most spectacular single episode was the advance by US First Army and the seizure of the Ludendorff bridge over the Rhine at Remagen by a platoon from US 9th Armored Division on 7 March. As a result the Americans were able to establish a foothold on the east bank. Von Rundstedt, who had once more been reappointed Commander in Chief in the West in September 1944, was once more dismissed by Hitler. The capture of other bridgeheads at Boppard and Oppenheim by 24 March, finally meant that the main Allied effort would be made in the center and south rather than in the north. In any case, enabling Montgomery to go for Berlin would have totally immobilized the other Allied armies when Berlin lacked any intrinsic military – as opposed to political – value. It had been allocated to the Soviet zone of occupation by agreement at the Yalta Conference in February 1945 and Eisenhower was far more concerned to prevent any last Nazi stand in the mountains of the south and Austria.

The crossing of the Rhine – Operation Varsity – began with a British attack below Duisburg on 24 March and involved a preparatory assault by over 21,000 airborne troops of XVIII Airborne Corps, which again suffered disproportionately heavy losses to little purpose. With the Americans breaking out of their bridgeheads simultaneously, the Ruhr was surrounded by 1 April when Allied pincers closed on Lippstadt. Although fighting continued for another month and was occasionally hard and bitter, the campaign in the west was virtually over and became a triumphant procession. Organized German resistance collapsed, the defenders often being only too anxious to surrender to the western Allies rather than to the Soviets. Model refused to surrender in the Ruhr pocket and dis-

Yalta and Potsdam

The majority of the great wartime conferences involved only the western powers and it was not until the Tehran Conference in November 1943 that Churchill, Roosevelt and Stalin met together. While they were most concerned with the prosecution of the war the three leaders did discuss aspects of a postwar settlement. There were early indications of differences, notably on the question of the political fate of a defeated Germany and on the precise future frontier between Poland and the Soviet Union. Nevertheless, the conference ended in reasonable harmony although the Polish Government-in-exile in London was incensed by the agreement at Tehran to move the Soviet border westward to the so-called Curzon Line.

By the time the three men met again at Yalta in February 1945 the situation was very different since Germany was now clearly close to defeat and the shape of the postwar world was of immediate and pressing importance. Stalin wanted Germany severely punished with $ 20 billion worth of reparations and he wanted Germany partitioned. Churchill and Roosevelt favored neither course and matters were left for further discussion. Another issue revived was that of Poland's frontiers. Churchill and Roosevelt accepted the Curzon Line as the Soviet western frontier but refused to accede to Stalin's demand to push the Polish western frontier up to the Oder and Neisse rivers to include a large German population. Stalin agreed to the inclusion of members of the London-based Polish Government in the so-called Lublin Committee established by the Soviets in Poland and gave an assurance that free elections would be held. But the western leaders were prepared to fudge on the future of eastern Europe because of their need to get Stalin into the war against Japan. Stalin gave his agreement to declaring war on Japan once Germany was defeated but only at the further price of being awarded the territories lost by Imperial Russia after her defeat by Japan in the Russo-Japanese War of 1904-05 and the Kurile islands Russia had ceded to Japan in 1875.

It soon became clear that the Soviets had little intention of adhering to the Yalta agreements, such as they were, as the Red Army imposed Soviet control over eastern Europe. Churchill now urged a stand against the Soviets but Truman, who had succeeded Roosevelt, still hoped that Stalin could be persuaded to show restraint. A new conference was necessary and Truman met with Churchill and Stalin at Potsdam in July only for Churchill to be replaced midway by Clement Attlee whose Labor Party had defeated Churchill in the British general election. Stalin would not be moved and the dropping of the atomic bombs during the Potsdam Conference was interpreted by the Soviets as a threat to themselves rather than as a means of ending the war against Japan. When the conference broke up in August it was clear that the wartime alliance was at an end.

LEFT: *US infantrymen advance through the German town of Prum.*

ABOVE: *Montgomery reading the surrender terms to representatives of the German forces in Denmark, Norway and northwest Germany at Lüneberg, 4 May 1945.*

RIGHT: *Maintaining the momentum of the Allied advance through Germany.*

solved Army Group B before committing suicide: 317,000 German troops fell into Allied hands.

One by one the great historic towns of Germany fell. Magdeburg on the Elbe was taken on 12 April, the day Roosevelt died and was succeeded as President by Harry S Truman. The Canadian First Army reached the North Sea on 16 April and US forces entered Czechoslovakia on the following day. They reached Torgau on 25 April and made contact with Soviet forces two days later. The Soviets had meanwhile completed their investment of Berlin and began the final attack on 28 April. Hitler, who had celebrated his 56th birthday on 20 April, named Admiral Doenitz as his successor and, with his mistress Eva Braun, took his own life on 30 April. The two bodies were burned in the garden of the Chancellery to be found by Soviet troops on 2 May. Berlin and the German forces in Italy surrendered on the same day.

Eisenhower having decided to halt on the Elbe, Montgomery received the surrender of all German forces in Denmark, the Netherlands, and northwest Germany at Lüneberg Heath on 4 May. Three days later, Field Marshal Keitel and General Jodl represented Doenitz at the formal surrender ceremony at Rheims in the presence of Air Chief Marshal Tedder representing Eisenhower and Zhukov representing the Soviets. Surrender became effective at 1101 on 8 May 1945. The European war was at an end.

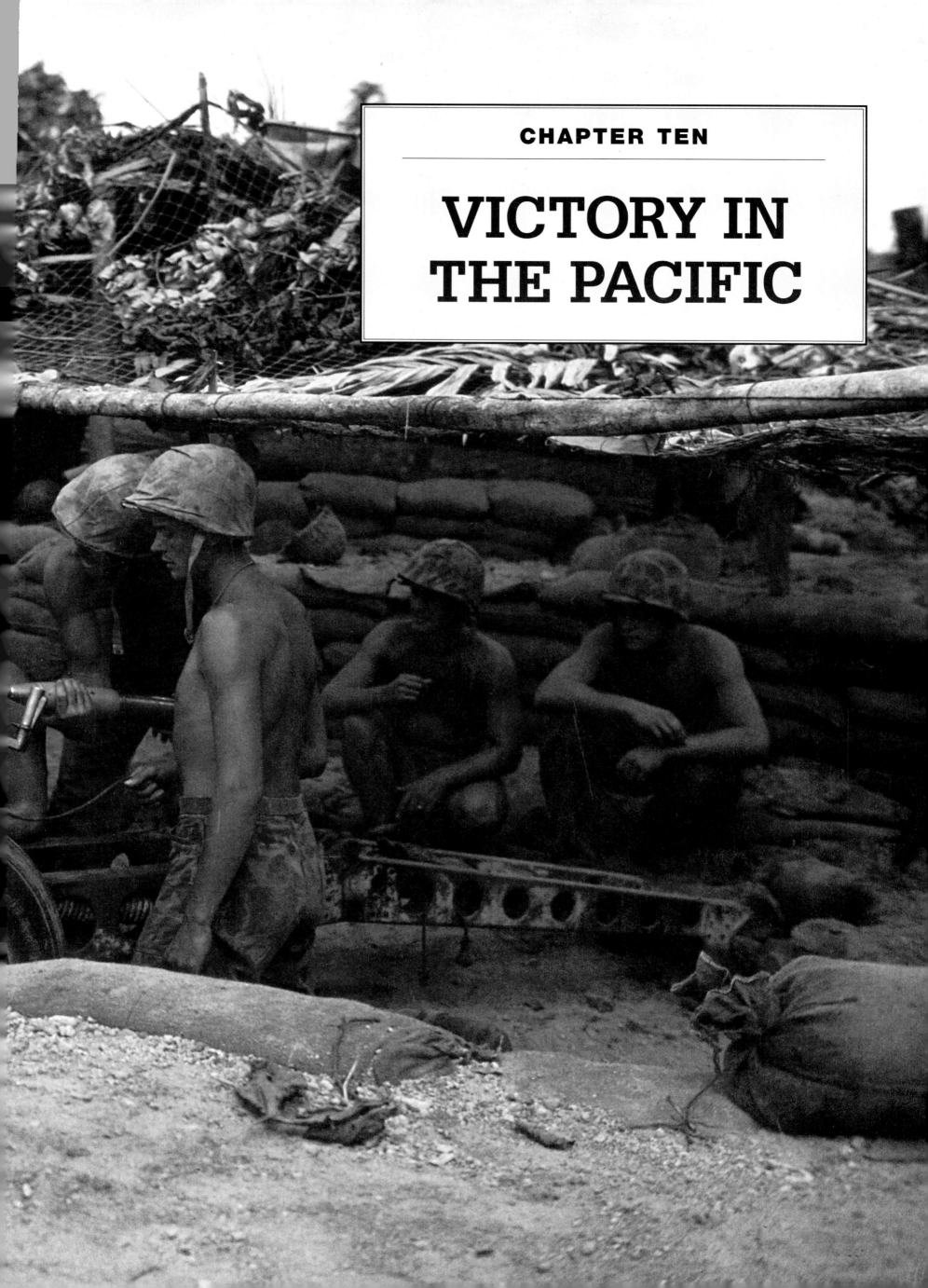

CHAPTER TEN

VICTORY IN THE PACIFIC

Going to war in search of a defendable perimeter from which to negotiate, the Japanese had experienced enormous successes which were to cost them dear in the long term. Tojo, who had become Prime Minister in October 1941 and had also taken five other ministerial portfolios in his own hands, now wanted to expand beyond the limited perimeter envisaged by Yamamoto and the Combined Fleet Staff. Tojo failed to recognize the contradictions between his ambitions for a Japanese 'Greater East Asia Co-prosperity Sphere' and the realities of Japanese resources and capabilities. The Army General Staff was more cautious but wanted to seize the Aleutians. Yamamoto was also interested in doing something rather than simply yielding initiative to the Allies and his staff toyed with a descent upon Ceylon while the Navy General Staff pressed strongly for the capture of the Gilbert, Bismarck, and Solomon islands before sweeping southeastward through New Guinea to Australia. The army was prepared to go as far as New Guinea but vetoed any attempt on Ceylon or Australia.

By April 1942 the advance to the southeast was well under way as 'victory disease' acquired a momentum all its own. At this moment, however, the US aircraft carriers absent from Pearl Harbor launched a dramatic raid, 16 B-25s led by Lieutenant Colonel Doolittle bombing Tokyo, Nagoya, Kobe, and Osaka on 18 April. It was an enormous jolt to the Japanese and brought the Navy General Staff to agree with Yamamoto that the first priority must now be taking on the American carriers. The chosen battleground was Midway.

The US Pacific Fleet, now commanded by Admiral Chester Nimitz, had been tasked with preventing the Japanese entering the eastern Pacific and had conducted a number of forays with this in mind in January and February 1942. Similarly, the Japanese carriers had undertaken further operations in support of amphibious landings as well as raids. Aircraft from the Japanese 1st Air Fleet bombed both Darwin in Australia on 19 February and Colombo and Trincomalee in Ceylon on 5 and 9 April respectively. They also sank the Royal Navy carrier HMS *Hermes* off Ceylon while other aircraft from a Japanese light carrier bombed the east coast of India in March. The carriers *Shoho*, *Shokaku*, and *Zuikaku* were then deployed in support of projected operations to capture Port Moresby in New Guinea.

Radio intercepts had alerted the Americans to the threat to Port Moresby and Nimitz ordered the carriers USS *Lexington* and *Yorktown* into the Coral Sea to meet the Japanese, *Yorktown* rendezvousing with *Lexington* on 5 May. On 7 and 8 May aircraft from the opposing fleets found and launched attacks on each other in this first carrier versus carrier clash. Both *Shoho* and *Lexington* were lost while the *Shokaku* was sufficiently badly damaged to need to return to Japan for repairs, and the Japanese were also forced to abandon the proposed attack on Port Moresby.

The loss of the *Shoho* made no difference to Yamamoto's plans for the Midway operation, the island being of vital strategic importance for the Americans since it guarded the approaches to Hawaii. Yamamoto planned to divert American attention toward the Aleutians then raid Midway with his fast carrier fleet and draw in the US carriers on both his own vessels and the main Japanese battle fleet in a decisive naval engagement. However, Nimitz knew the Japanese intentions through the work of his code breakers and refused to be drawn by the Aleutians diversion. Thus, when the Japanese approached Midway on 3 June, they were hit by land-based aircraft from the island. In turn, the Japanese launched a devastating air attack on Midway on the following day but were then competely surprised by the appearance of American carrier aircraft from USS *Enterprise*, *Yorktown* and *Hornet*. All four carriers in Vice-Admiral Nagumo's 1st Carrier

PREVIOUS PAGES: *US artillerymen prepare to fire their howitzer during the fighting on Bougainville.*

TOP LEFT: *One of the B-25s of Doolittle's raid takes off from the USS* Hornet *for Japan, 18 April 1942.*

CENTER LEFT: *A direct hit on a Japanese Shokaku class carrier by aircraft from USS* Yorktown *during the Battle of the Coral Sea, 8 May 1942.*

ABOVE: *US aircraft on the deck of the USS* Yorktown *during the Coral Sea operations.*

LEFT: *An explosion seals the fate of the USS* Lexington, *blowing one aircraft off its deck during the Battle of the Coral sea.*

RIGHT: *The Japanese cruiser* Mikuma *abandoned and sinking after being hit by aircraft from USS* Enterprise *during the Midway battle, 6 June, 1942. Torpedoes hang from the portside tubes.*

Striking Force – *Akagi, Kaga, Soryu,* and *Hiryu* – were to be sunk and Yamamoto was forced to order a general retirement. Next day *Yorktown* survived severe damage from aircraft from the *Hiryu* but the carrier was then sunk by a Japanese submarine on 6 June. Yamamoto had lost his decisive battle and with it Japan's superiority in naval strength. He himself was to be shot down and killed en route to Bougainville from Truk on 18 April 1943 after the Americans had intercepted his announced itinerary.

While the United States Joint Chiefs of Staff had made the defeat of Germany rather than that of Japan their first priority, both the US Navy led by its Commander in Chief, Admiral King, and MacArthur, commanding Southeast Pacific Area from Australia, were determined to strike back at the Japanese. King and MacArthur recognized the need to retake Rabaul on New Britain which had provided the Japanese with a firm base for any operations against New Guinea and the Solomons. However, they differed on how to achieve this object and Washington had to rule on Nimitz moving into the southern Solomons in August 1942 to be followed by MacArthur directing operations to seize the remainder of the Solomons and Rabaul itself.

Accordingly, while Nimitz prepared for a thrust at Guadalcanal in the Solomons, MacArthur moved to secure Port Moresby as a base for his own endeavors. Australian forces moved there in May and June 1942 and in early July began advancing over the Kokoda Trail through the Owen Stanley Mountains towards Buna. But, having been thwarted in their seaborne attempt on Port Moresby, the Japanese had resolved on an overland advance with troops from Seventeenth Army landing at Buna on 21 July. A savage struggle ensued which was to cost the lives of 13,000 Japanese and over 3000 Australians and Americans before Buna finally fell to the Allies on 2 January 1943. Equal difficulties faced the 19,000 US Marines from 1st Marine Division landed on Guadalcanal on 7 August 1942. The initial landing was unopposed but there was heavy opposition on neighboring islands and the Japanese were able to reinforce Guadalcanal itself later in August. Indeed, it was not until 8 February 1943 that the Japanese withdrew after the Americans had diverted two divisions previously earmarked for Europe to the Pacific. In inflicting 24,000 casualties on the Japanese compared to 6300 of their own, the Americans had been able to defeat the Japanese on land for the first time.

ABOVE LEFT: Wreckage and supplies lie on Kwajalein in the Marshalls after its capture, February 1944.

TOP RIGHT: American Under Secretary for the Navy, James Forrestal (left), visits a captured airfield on the Solomons.

ABOVE RIGHT: The chief torpedoman on USS O'Bannon *checking quintuple torpedo tubes during the Solomons operations.*

LEFT: A Marine patrol in a Pacific jungle.

RIGHT: F-4 Corsairs on Guadalcanal.

The Guadalcanal campaign was also marked by fierce naval battles in the narrow waters around the islands, the Japanese making good use of the cover of night to inflict losses on Allied cruisers and destroyers. Five Allied ships were lost on 8 August 1942 alone off Savo. The carriers USS *Wasp* and *Hornet* were also lost in September and October respectively. However, the Japanese did lose the carrier *Ryujo* in August and the *Shokaku* was crippled for a second time in October. The battleships *Kirishimà* and *Hiei* also went down to the guns of the USS *Washington* and *South Dakota* in November 1942.

Securing Guadalcanal and Buna cleared the way for further operations in the Solomons and New Guinea during 1943 with the intention of tackling Rabaul during 1944. However, despite the opposition of MacArthur, it was also decided to mount a separate advance across the central Pacific through the Gilbert and Marshall islands and to eject the Japanese from the Aleutians. The British expressed some concern at Casablanca in January 1943 that the ambitious nature of the program would divert resources from the defeat of Germany and some modifications were agreed at the Trident Conference in May 1943 and at Quebec in August. By then MacArthur had begun his operations by moving in late June 1943 to seize Lae and Salamaua in New Guinea while naval forces allocated to him but directed by Admiral William Halsey began landing the US 43rd Infantry Division on New Georgia. The Japanese were forced to evacuate the island on 20 August and Halsey's forces then leapfrogged to Treasury island and Choiseul in October before the 3rd Marine Division was put ashore on Bougainville on 1 November.

The fighting through the Solomons was often fierce and there were also further clashes between opposing aircraft and fleets. By 26 December, however, Japanese airfields on Bougainville had been captured and US aircraft based there were able to start launching raids on Rabaul. Australian and US troops had also made good progress in their advance along the New Guinea coast, the Australian 9th Division repulsing attempted Japanese counterattacks in October 1943 and inflicting heavy losses. Rabaul was effectively neutralized and the Japanese pulled their fleet

ABOVE: Marines cautiously probe forward toward a US tank disabled at the junction of the Piva and Numa-Numa tracks on Bougainville, 14 November 1943.

RIGHT: Soldiers of the US 43rd Infantry Division taking cover after coming ashore on Rendova, New Georgia, August 1944.

TOP RIGHT: Dead Japanese defenders on Guadalcanal in the Solomons, December 1942.

LEFT: PBJ bombers of the USMC raid Rabaul in 1943.

RIGHT: The end for one of the defenders of Bougainville, November 1943.

back as the Allies landed on New Britain. Fighting in New Guinea and the southwest Pacific continued until May 1944 but clearing the Solomons and New Britain had opened the way to the Philippines.

The Quadrant Conference had settled that the central Pacific drive under Nimitz must commence with an assault on the Gilberts in November 1943, to be followed by operations against the Marshalls in January 1944 and the Carolines in June. These series of islands – mostly coral atolls – were required in order to push forward the reach of Allied aircraft toward the Philippines, mainland China and Japan itself. Unfortunately for the Americans,

Amphibious Operations

Amphibious assault became a new specialization during the war with specialized new craft such as LCTs (Landing Craft Tanks) and LSTs (Landing Ship Tanks) and highly complex planning and organization. Much was learned from Operation Torch in North Africa in November 1942 and 'Husky' on Sicily in July 1943, when many of the new craft were used on a large scale for the first time. Operations Overlord and Dragoon in Normandy and southern France respectively in 1944 were also major undertakings which saw further refinements of the techniques applied in North Africa and Sicily. Similar developments also occurred in the Pacific where the formative experience was the landing on Tarawa in November 1943. Lessons learned there were then applied to landings in the Marshalls. Here LCI(G)s (Landing Craft Infantry, Gunships) with rapid-firing cannon and rockets; LVTs (Landing Vehicles Tracked) or troop-carrying amphibious tractors; LVT(A)s or armored amphibian tanks; and the celebrated DUKWs (amphibious transports) first made their appearance. The United States Navy also evolved a sophsticated method of integrating the actions of a variety of naval task groups for bombardment, transport, floating supply, fire support, air support, salvage, and actual assault which were required to put a self-sufficient force ashore thousands of miles from the nearest land bases.

Amphibious tractors heading for Tarawa.

while the Japanese could spare few additional resources for the defense of these islands, they had worked hard to fortify them with bunkers and other strongpoints and were determined to hold them to the last. Thus, when US 2nd Marine Division assaulted Tarawa and the 27th Infantry Division landed on Makin on 20 November 1943, they discovered that heavy naval bombardment had not subdued the defenders. Makin was secured without heavy casualties but the marines ran into heavy opposition on 'Bloody Tarawa.' Tackling the bunkers proved slow and costly, especially as the marines had only light weapons until tanks were put ashore later. By the time Tarawa was secured on 25 November only 146 out of a Japanese garrison of 4836 men were still alive and most of the survivors were Korean laborers rather than Japanese troops. The marines had suffered over 1000 dead and over 2000 wounded in their first major amphibious assault. However, the lessons learned were applied to succeeding operations in the Marshalls in January and February 1944. Some of the stronger garrisons were by-passed but landings were made on Majuro (30 January), Kwajalein (1 February) and Eniwetok (18 February). The Japanese bases at Ponape and Truk were subjected to air attack, 137,091 tons of Japanese merchant shipping and 15 warships being sent to the bottom at Truk on 17 and 18 February 1944.

BELOW: *An F-64F Hellcat making a hard landing on the USS* Cowpens *during the operations in the Gilberts, November 1943.*

RIGHT: *Pilots being briefed on the USS* Lexington *during the Gilberts operations.*

BELOW RIGHT: *The beach on 'Bloody Tarawa,' 20 November 1943.*

1943 had also seen the beginnings of British attempts to return to Burma. Having been bundled out of Burma in May 1942, the first task had been to rebuild the army. No better man could have been tasked with doing so than Lieutenant General William Slim who had extricated Burma Corps in the closing months of the retreat with consumate skill. In the remaining months of 1942 Slim began to restore morale and start a reorganization which was to culminate in the formation of IV and XV Corps in August 1943 into a newly designated British Fourteenth Army. Particular attention was given to medical support and to preventing diseases prevalent in the jungle such as malaria, dysentery, and mite typhus. Mepacrine and other new drugs became available but it was also a matter of strict health discipline. A massive logistic build-up was also required since the traditional threat to India had been that of Russian invasion across the Northwest Frontier, and the pattern and direction of India's strategic railways and roads reflected this consideration. Assam in the northeast was served only by a single track railway from Calcutta built for the seasonal jute trade. New communications, pipelines and six new airfields had to be constructed, including a 275-mile oil pipeline to connect Bombay with the Assam railway. Calcutta's docks also had to be completely reconstructed by March 1944.

Another important consideration for Slim was to demonstrate that his troops could meet and beat the Japanese in the jungle. However, matters were complicated by the civil disobedience campaign mounted by Indian nationalists which led to troops being kept in India. Wavell as Supreme Commander was therefore unable to contemplate any major offensive before late 1943 but did agree to a limited advance against Japanese airfields at Akyab in Arakan. It had been intended to stage an amphibious assault on Akyab but landing craft and troops were required for the campaign against the Vichy French on Madagascar between May and November 1942. Wavell decided to go ahead with a land advance only but this first Arakan campaign was a failure. Launched in September 1942, British and Indian troops reached the line Buthidaung to Maungdaw by December but the Japanese reinforced the Arakan and the advance got bogged down in stubborn fighting around Donbaik and Rathedaung between January and March 1943.

A second effort to take the offensive took the form of a

The Chindits

The troublesome and unorthodox Orde Wingate arrived in Burma in March 1942 as a 38-year-old major. Immediately promoted to colonel, and eventually to major general, he was posted to the 'Bush Warfare School' at Maymyo. It was there that he formulated his concept for long-range penetration operations, and as a result 77th Indian Infantry Brigade was established to put the idea into action. Some 2200 men were directed to attack the Mandalay to Myitkyina railway between Nankan and Bongyaung while a further 1000 men struck the same line at Kyaikthin. While Wingate did manage to sabotage the railway between February and March 1943 and to prove that formations could be successfully supplied by air in the jungle, his decision to press beyond the Irrawaddy was foolhardy. Forced to retreat by privation and Japanese attacks, the 77th Brigade sustained almost 1000 casualties and nearly all those that did return were lost for all future operations. Despite the limited success, Wingate was lionized by the press, a *Daily Express* journalist coining the name 'Chindits' from the Burmese word for lion. Wingate also caught Churchill's imagination, and at the Quebec Conference in July 1943 won approval for a much more ambitious penetration. The plan had to be scaled down but Wingate was still able to deploy five brigades – the 14th, 16th, 77th, 111th, and 3rd West African Brigades – for his second expedition to assist Stilwell's advance on Myitkyina. Immense difficulties were encountered flying the men into the jungle by glider, and Wingate's expectation that his men could hold jungle airstrips and operate almost as conventional forces for long periods in the Japanese rear proved erroneous. The Chindits suffered over 3600 casualties although it can be argued that they diverted Japanese resources and caused considerable confusion in the Japanese rear at a key moment in the Burma campaign. Wingate himself died in an air crash at an early stage of the second expedition.

LEFT: *Japanese bicycle troops crossing a bridge during the Burma campaign.*

CENTER LEFT: *Men of Calvert's Chindit column preparing a bridge for demolition at the 'White City' position during the second Wingate expedition, March 1944.*

deep penetration of Japanese lines beyond the Chindwin by Wingate's Chindits between February and June 1943. Orde Wingate had made his reputation in Palestine before the war when he had organized the Jewish Special Night Squads to defend Jewish settlements and communications against Arab terrorists. He had also enjoyed success in mounting guerrilla operations against the Italians in Ethiopia and Wavell, who had known Wingate in Palestine, specifically asked for his services. The Chindits, who were chosen from Wingate's 77th Indian Brigade, cut the Mandalay to Myitkyina railway in no less than 75 places in March 1943 but their losses were heavy. Only 600 of the 2182 men committed were ever fit enough to serve again. The real value lay in the demonstration of the ability of Allied troops to move through the jungle when supplied by air and also it assisted in boosting morale.

Any wider offensive against the Japanese would require the co-operation of the Nationalist Chinese whose Fifth and Sixth Armies had been used in Burma in 1942 in a vain attempt to keep open the Burma Road. At Casablanca in January 1943 the Allies decided that the first priority in Burma must be to re-open land communications between the British and Chinese, a decision confirmed at both Trident and Quadrant conferences although there were some differences of opinion about whether it was necessary to clear all of Burma. A new Southeast Asia Command was created in August 1943 under Vice-Admiral Lord Louis Mountbatten in order to co-ordinate British, Chinese and American efforts. The Americans were heavily committed to propping up Chiang Kai-shek and his Chief of Staff was the American Lieutenant General Joseph Stilwell. Mountbatten directed that an offensive should be mounted in November 1943 with the object of clearing northern Burma so that the Ledo Road from Assam could be linked to the old Burma Road at Lashio. Myitkyina would also have to be secured to allow further expansion of the United States' aerial resupply of China over the 'Hump.'

Stilwell was tasked with advancing on Myitkyina while British XV Corps pushed down the Arakan toward Akyab and Wingate led another deep penetration operation to disrupt Japanese communications and help Stilwell's advance. XV Corps was strongly counterattacked by the Japanese as expected but, drawing on the lesson of the first Wingate expedition, they held fast when the

Japanese cut their lines of communication and were supplied by air. By May 1944 the Japanese were in retreat themselves. Stilwell, whose advance was greatly assisted by the performance of the American unit known as Merrill's Marauders, took the vital airfield at Myitkyina on 17 May but was unable to clear the town until 3 August. In the process, the Marauders suffered heavily and all but collapsed. Meanwhile, drawing on the manpower of six brigades, Wingate's force was airlanded into northern Burma in March 1944 to block communications between Mandalay and Myitkyina around Indaw and Mawlu. Wingate himself was killed in an air crash on 25 March and, facing increasingly heavy opposition, the Chindits retired northward to Mogaung in April. They were forced out of Mogaung as well at the end of May but the Japanese did not react quickly enough to exploit the opportunity and Stilwell's Chinese took the town on 26 June.

Paradoxically, the first Wingate expedition had also convinced the Japanese that Burma's northern hills were not as impenetrable as they had supposed. The Allied offensive thus coincided with a major Japanese offensive by Fifteenth Army in Assam – the 'March on Delhi' – which aimed to break into the Brahmaputra valley before pushing into eastern India. The Japanese also launched a new offensive in eastern China (Operation *Ichi-go*) to take advantage of the Nationalist Chinese commitment in Burma. This was not finally halted until December 1944.

Slim had anticipated the Japanese offensive, which began on 15 March 1944, and IV Corps fell back as planned on Imphal and Kohima. When the Japanese cut the Imphal road on 29 March it isolated four divisions while two more were cut off around Kohima, the initial defense of which between 5 and 18 April was conducted by 4th Battalion, Queen's Own Royal West Kents. At one stage only the width of the local District Commissioner's tennis court separated the British and Japanese positions. As in the Arakan, Imphal and Kohima were supplied by air although in order to do so Mountbatten had to obtain 79 C-47 Dakotas from the Middle East which he refused to return until 1 July. The Indian 5th Division was flown in to Imphal from the Arakan as reinforcements and British XXXIII Corps led by British 2nd Division was able to begin pushing toward Kohima. British 6th Brigade relieved the West Kents on 18 April but it was not until 3 June that the place was fully relieved. XXXIII Corps then pushed on to

BOTTOM, FAR LEFT: *Arguably the greatest British commander of the war – Lieutenant General Sir William Slim photographed on 5 March 1945.*

BELOW: *Lieutenant General Joseph Stilwell (seated center) confers with one of his Chinese divisional commanders in northern Burma.*

BELOW RIGHT: *Japanese troops carrying artillery sections in northwest Burma.*

Imphal, 2nd Division linking with the garrison there on 22 June. The Japanese themselves had undertaken the offensive without sufficient logistic back-up and they broke under the strain of British counterattacks. By 19 August 1944 the Japanese had been forced out of Assam altogether.

At the Cairo and Tehran Conferences in December 1943 the Allies had further refined the overall strategic plan by establishing the Pacific as the clear second theater to northwest Europe, the Mediterranean and Burma being thrust firmly to the bottom of the priority list. It had also been accepted that the next target in the Pacific would be the Marianas from which B-29s could reach the Japanese homeland. Subsequently, MacArthur would be able to continue operations against the Philippines with a tentative date of November 1944 set for a landing on the southern island of Mindanao. Nimitz also hoped to entice the Japanese Fleet into an engagement.

In fact, while the Japanese failed to perceive the Marianas as the next likely American target, they had formulated plans for using their carriers to lure away the US carriers and then attack the American invasion force with their main battle fleet. The Americans were aware of the risk and when the US 2nd and 4th Marine Divisions began landing on Saipan in the Marianas on 15 June 1944, Vice-Admiral Spruance kept his 12 carriers as close to the beachhead as possible. Four days later when the Japanese threw 430 aircraft at the Pacific Fleet, only 102 survived with a further 50 land-based Japanese aircraft also being lost. Moreover, the Americans sank the carriers *Shokaku*, *Taiho*, and *Hiyo* and crippled the *Zuikaku* and *Chiyoda* before the Japanese withdrew on 20 June. What was known officially as the Battle of the Philippines Sea, and more popularly among American pilots as the 'Great Marianas Turkey Shoot,' was the last and largest carrier battle of the war. It marked the effective end of the Japanese naval air arm and Admiral Nagumo committed suicide after the battle.

On land the two marine divisions were reinforced by 27th Infantry Division to secure Saipan by 9 July. The marines were then shifted to Tinian on 24 July, 2nd Marine Division making a diversionary feint off Tinian Town while the 4th went ashore in the north. The island was secured by 1 August although fanatical Japanese continued to emerge from hiding places to launch desperate attacks: the closing stages of the fighting on both Saipan and Tinian had also been characterized by mass suicides among both Japanese soldiers and civilians. The last objective in the Marianas – Guam – was also the most

TOP LEFT: Grim trophies of the Allied pursuit of the Japanese to the Chindwin, Burma, July 1944.

ABOVE LEFT: Men of the 4th Marine Division hurling grenades at Japanese positions on Saipan, June 1944.

LEFT: Japanese cruisers and transports off Orote Point, Guam, July 1944.

RIGHT: *Crew members of the USS* New Mexico *line up for a meal during a lull in the fighting around the island of Guam.*

BELOW: *The* New Mexico *back in action off Guam. Its main guns blast away at a long-range land target.*

important because of its excellent anchorage and the assault there began on 21 July with 3rd Marine Division landing at Asan and 1st Marine Brigade reinforced by 77th Infantry Division at Agat. The now customary *banzai* counterattacks were encountered but Guam was declared secure on 10 August although the last Japanese soldier did not emerge to surrender until 1960. The Marianas campaign had cost over 22,000 American casualties and the Japanese over 60,000, the majority of whom were killed or committed suicide. Japan itself was now open to direct attack, a fact recognized in Tokyo where Tojo's government had fallen on 18 July 1944.

Allied planning had been sufficiently flexible to enable opportunities to be seized as they occurred and for resources to be switched between MacArthur and Nimitz if required. Unfortunately, a rift had developed between the advocates of the two strategies as Nimitz struck through the Marianas and moved on to the Carolines in September 1944 and MacArthur continued to advance through New Guinea. MacArthur was firmly committed to a triumphant return to the Philippines as the next objective but Admiral King believed that the war could be shortened by striking at Formosa. In the event, probing toward the Philippines by Halsey's 3rd Fleet indictated that the archipelago was much more weakly held than suspected and the decision was taken in September to bypass Mindanao and go straight for a landing in Leyte Gulf in October. It meant MacArthur would be able to go on to Luzon in December. Nimitz and King now proposed a change in the direction of the central Pacific advance toward Iwo Jima in the Bonins and Okinawa in the Ryukyus and this was agreed for early 1945.

Once more the Japanese attempted to retrieve the situation by naval action using carriers as bait, and the battle fleet against the American vessels supporting the operations which began at Leyte with US X and XXIV Corps of General Krueger's Sixth Army landing on 20 October 1944. The Japanese did succeed in drawing off Halsey's Third Fleet, but in the four major actions that constituted the Battle of Leyte Gulf between 23 and 25 October they still lost the battleships *Musashi*, *Fuso*, and *Yamashiro* and the carrier *Zuikaku*, the last survivor from the Pearl Harbor attack. In addition the Japanese also lost three light carriers, ten cruisers, and 11 destroyers. The Americans lost one light and two escort carriers and three destroyers. However, the Japanese battle fleet had suffered much the same fate as the carrier fleet and future operations were restricted by dwindling fuel supplies. With so many of the trained pilots lost, the Japanese now resorted to *kamikaze* ('divine wind') tactics to counter American naval superiority. The first such attack was experienced at Leyte on 25 October when the escort carrier USS *St Lo* was sunk.

LEFT: *A US flag is raised on a boat-hook mast as marines land on Guam, 21 July 1944.*

RIGHT: *An LST manned by the US Coastguard Service carrying supplies to Leyte Gulf.*

BELOW: *The Japanese battleship* Ise *under attack off Cape Engango, Leyte Gulf, 25 October 1944.*

BOTTOM LEFT: *Japanese troops lie dead after an unsuccessful counterattack on Saipan's Aslito airfield.*

BOTTOM: *A captured Japanese Yokosuka MXY-7 Ohka 'Cherry Blossom' suicide aircraft on Okinawa.*

BOTTOM RIGHT: *A kamikaze pilot dons a rising sun headband prior to a mission.*

BOTTOM, FAR RIGHT: *A Japanese 'Judy' kamikaze plane brought down by anti-aircraft fire from USS* Wasp *off the Ryukyus, 18 March 1945.*

LEFT: *Three GIs search ruined houses for Japanese snipers – a scene from the bitter fighting around Fort Stotesenberg on Luzon.*

BELOW LEFT: *US troops push deeper into the walled city of Intramuros on Luzon. Evidence of heavy fighting can be seen on the ruined facade of the city's post office.*

TOP RIGHT: *USS* Nevada *bombarding Iwo Jima, February 1945.*

ABOVE RIGHT: *Marine Lieutenant General Holland Smith and Major General Schmidt outside V Amphibious Corps Headquarters, Iwo Jima.*

RIGHT: *The official flag raising ceremony on Iwo Jima, 14 March 1945.*

FAR RIGHT: *The British reconquest of Burma, 1944-45.*

More losses were inflicted by the suicide attacks when the Americans continued the conquest of the Philippines by landing at Mindoro on 15 December 1944 and at Lingayen Gulf on Luzon on 9 January 1945. On 6 January alone 16 Allied ships including the battleship USS *New Mexico* were hit: the Australian cruiser HMAS *Australia* was hit that day for a third time. *Kaiten* suicide boats were also used and on land the fighting was equally hard,

Krueger's Sixth Army suffering over 15,000 casualties on Leyte between October 1944 and May 1945. On Luzon Krueger's troops and those of Lieutenant General Eichelberger's US Eighth Army took 37,000 casualties while the Japanese, directed by Yamashita, the victor of Malaya and Singapore, lost over 205,000 from a garrison of 275,000. Manila was virtually laid waste in the struggle. Eichelberger then went on to clear the remainder of the

Philippines between February and July 1945, and no less than 52 separate landing operations were required. Lieutenant General Morshead's Australian I Corps also began mopping up in Borneo prior to an expected push into the Dutch East Indies.

In Burma, Slim's Fourteenth Army had continued to harry the Japanese throughout the monsoon, crossing the Chindwin in pursuit of the Japanese in early December 1944. The Chinese continued to strive to open the Burma Road and finally did so on 20 January 1945. To the west XV Corps had attacked in the Arakan on 12 December and took Akyab on 4 January, 3 Commando Brigade landing from the sea at Kangaw on 22 January to cut Japanese communications. A further amphibious assault was mounted against the Japanese positions on Ramree Island in February. Airfields in the Arakan could now be used to supply Slim in central Burma where the Japanese attempted to hold a line from Mandalay to Lashio. With tremendous skill, Slim changed his plans and diverted the attention of the Japanese to Mandalay while throwing IV Corps across the Irrawaddy to the south after complicated maneuvers between 13 and 21 February. Meiktilia was taken on 3 March to cut the Japanese line of retreat. Lieutenant General Kimura attempted a counterattack then ran for Toungoo. Mandalay fell to the British on 20 March 1945 and British-led Karen tribesmen got to Toungoo first to nullify Kimura's intentions. Kimura attempted a further stand at Pegu but was again pushed back. XV Corps then mounted an operation to seize Rangoon before the onset of the monsoon and the city fell without much opposition to amphibious assault by the Indian 26th Division on 3 May. While mopping up operations were to continue until August 1945, the Burma campaign was over.

Delayed by the need to support MacArthur's operations in the Philippines, Nimitz landed on Iwo Jima on 19 February 1945, the island again being a required forward base for bombers operating against Japan. The Japanese had been working on the defenses for almost eight months and in taking an island of only 11.25 square miles the three marine divisions used in the assault lost 566

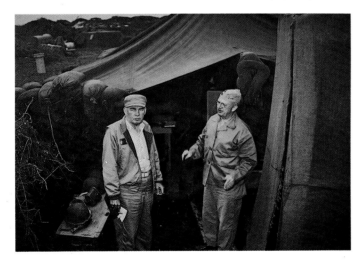

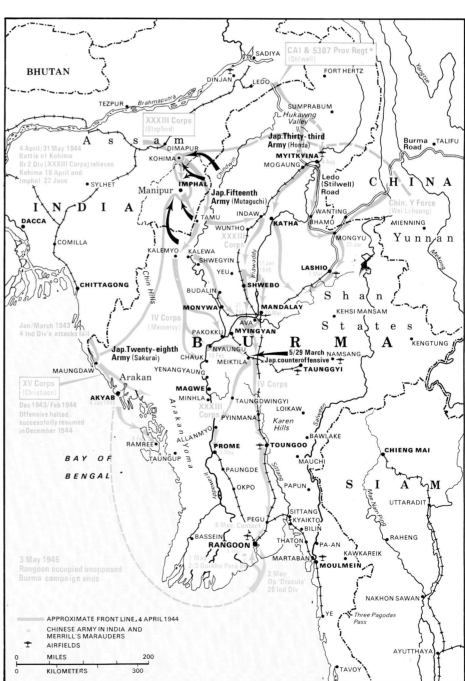

LEFT: *Douglas MacArthur returns to the Philippines, 25 October 1944.*

BELOW: *Men of the 5th Marine Division working their way up Red Beach on Iwo Jima, 19 February 1945.*

TOP RIGHT: *Troops from the 6th Marine Division flushing Japanese out of a cane field on Okinawa with smoke grenades, 13 June 1945. One Japanese can be seen emerging at center.*

RIGHT: *Men of the 5th Marine Division pose with a captured Japanese flag on Iwo Jima, 23 February 1945.*

BELOW RIGHT: *An amphibious tractor of the 2nd Marine Division leaving an LST bound for Iheya, 6 March 1945.*

BELOW, FAR RIGHT: *The end of a suicide mission as the Japanese battleship Yamato explodes, 7 April 1945.*

dead and 1755 wounded just coming ashore. Only 1083 out of the Japanese garrison of 23,000 were taken alive and total marine casualties from an assaulting force of 30,000 men ran at 30 percent. The garrison of Okinawa was over 90,000 strong and Lieutenant General Buckner's US Tenth Army was allocated for the operation to subdue this next American target. US III Amphibious Corps and XXIV Corps landed on the west coast on 1 April and 2nd Marine Division on the east. Once more the Japanese had massed *kamikaze* and *kaiten*, and the battleship *Yamato* was also despatched on a suicide mission with just enough fuel to reach Okinawa. Since the loss of her sister ship *Musashi* at Leyte, the *Yamato* was the largest and most powerful battleship afloat. But she never got to fire her 45.8cm main armament in anger, for repeated US aerial attacks on 4 April sank her in the Van Diemen Strait. *Kamikazes* took out 21 Allied ships and crippled 43 others between 6 April and 22 June while the land fighting proved to be one of the costliest operations of the Pacific war with over 12,000 dead and 36,000 wounded among both Allied soldiers and seamen. The Japanese lost another 110,000 dead and over 4000 aircraft including almost 2000 shot down during *kamikaze* missions.

The pressure on Japan was also increasing in other ways. US submarines had been wreaking havoc with the Japanese merchant fleet. It was reduced from a peak of 5.5 million tons in mid-1942 to barely 1.5 million tons by August 1945. In the last year of the war a concentrated attack was begun on Japanese tankers on which her economy depended. At the same time, Japan was exposed to air bombardment. Bombing of the homeland began from the bases the Americans established on the Marianas in November 1944 using the new B-29 Superfortresses. The first targets were Japanese aircraft factories but in February 1945 the Americans switched to fire raids on major centers using incendiaries. On the night of 9 March the raid on Tokyo resulted in 83,793 deaths and the same treatment was meted out to other cities in succeeding months. The strategic bombing of Japan undoubtedly strengthened a more moderate faction within the Japanese leadership which now wanted peace but there was still every likelihood of appalling Allied casualties – perhaps as high as a million – if the Allies were compelled to invade Japan to end the war. That invasion (Operation Downfall) was now scheduled to begin with a landing on Kyushu in November 1945 ('Olympic') and on Honshu ('Coronet') in March 1946.

However, other developments were to intervene. The Manhattan Project – the development of an atomic bomb – reached its testing phase in mid-1945. On 1 June the so-called Interim Committee recommended using the bomb and on 16 July it was successfully tested in the New Mexico desert. Having given the Japanese an opportunity to respond to surrender terms agreed among the Allies at the Potsdam Conference, President Truman authorized use of the bomb on 28 July. At 0811 on 6 August 1945 the B-29 *Enola Gay* dropped the first bomb, nicknamed 'Little Boy,' on Hiroshima. With the Japanese still unable to agree surrender, a second bomb, 'Fat Man,' was dropped on Nagasaki three days later.

While the dropping of the atomic bombs convinced Emperor Hirohito that peace was necessary, the military still resisted surrender. On the day before the second bomb hit Nagasaki, Stalin had finally adhered to pledges given at the Yalta Conference and declared war on Japan. Drawing on the lessons of the last four years the Red Army advanced into Japanese Manchuria in a model Soviet-style Blitzkrieg. The once much-vaunted Japanese Kwantung Army was smashed within days although Soviet

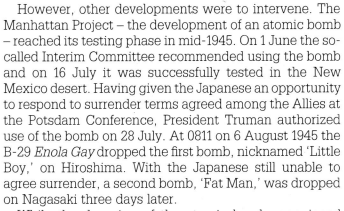

TOP LEFT: *Admirals Nimitz and Spruance (wearing sun helmet) visit Okinawa.*

CENTER, FAR LEFT: *USS Bunker Hill burning after being hit by a kamikaze off Okinawa, 11 May 1945.*

FAR LEFT: *Bombarding the mainland of Japan, 14 July 1945.*

ABOVE LEFT: *LST-829 off Okinawa, landing causeways lashed to its sides.*

LEFT: *Anti-aircraft lookouts on a US warship off Okinawa.*

TOP: *The atomic cloud rises over Nagasaki, 9 August 1945.*

TOP RIGHT: *The nuclear devastation of Nagasaki.*

ABOVE: *The business districts of Kobe, Japan, after the fire raids of February 1945.*

The Manhattan Project

The creation of the atomic bombs dropped on Hiroshima and Nagasaki was the culmination of a long series of key inventions by scientists stretching from the discovery of the X-ray in 1895 through Rutherford's splitting of the atom in 1919 to Otto Hahn's breakthrough in 1938 in discovering the fission process. Hahn's discovery raised enormous scientific interest and by 1939 scientists in Britain, France and the United States were beginning to investigate the military potential of nuclear energy. In Britain in particular work progressed to an extent which excited the Americans when it was revealed to them in mid-1941, and in October of that year Churchill and Roosevelt agreed to pool resources, the possibility that Germany might be attempting to produce a bomb first spurring action.

It became clear that only the United States had the necessary capabilities to make a bomb and this was agreed by the British in June 1942 when the Manhattan Project was formally established under the direction of Lieutenant General Leslie Groves. It enabled the simultaneous pursuit of five different possible alternative routes to producing a nuclear device.

Scientists such as Robert Oppenheimer, Enrico Fermi, Otto Frisch and Niels Bohr worked at a variety of sites including Oakridge in Tennessee, Hanford in Washington State, the University of Chicago and Los Alamos in New Mexico. After an expenditure of some $ 2000 million a bomb was successfully tested near Alamogordo in New Mexico on 16 July 1945.

The first bomb dropped ('Little Boy') weighed some 9000lbs but had the power of 20,000 tons of high explosive. Dropped over Hiroshima by the B-29 *Enola Gay* piloted by Colonel Paul W Tibbets, it generated a force of blast of 8.0 tons per square yard and an estimated heat at ground zero of 6000 deg. C. Estimates vary but it is thought that between 70,000 and 80,000 died at Hiroshima with 80,000 to 130,000 injured to varying degrees. The second bomb ('Fat Man') with similar characteristics to the first killed between 20,000 and 35,000 at Nagasaki and injured between 50,000 and 60,000 people. More had died in the fire raids on Tokyo and other cities, but these raids did not have the long-term implications of the release of radiation over Hiroshima and Nagasaki.

'Little Boy': the bomb dropped on Hiroshima, 6 August 1945.

operations were to continue until 20 August. Yet, the Japanese Army still refused to concede defeat even after the Soviets had entered the war and elements attempted a coup just before the emperor and his government surrendered on 15 August 1945. When the emperor broadcast the decision to his people, it was the first time they had ever heard his voice.

The official surrender ceremony to end the Pacific and Far Eastern war took place on the battleship USS *Missouri* in Tokyo Bay on 2 September 1945. Among those present as witnesses were Generals Percival and Wainwright who had been forced to capitulate to the Japanese almost four years previously at Singapore and Corregidor respectively. It was the final act in a drama which had proved to be the greatest and costliest conflict yet endured.

LEFT: *The* Enola Gay *takes off for Hiroshima.*

BELOW: *The Japanese commission signing the surrender terms on the USS* Missouri *in Tokyo Bay, 2 September 1945. MacArthur can be seen standing at left of the table with his back to the camera.*

RIGHT: *Japanese troops of the Kwantung Army pass into Soviet captivity.*

BELOW LEFT: *Soviet infantry cross the Manchurian frontier, 9 August 1945.*